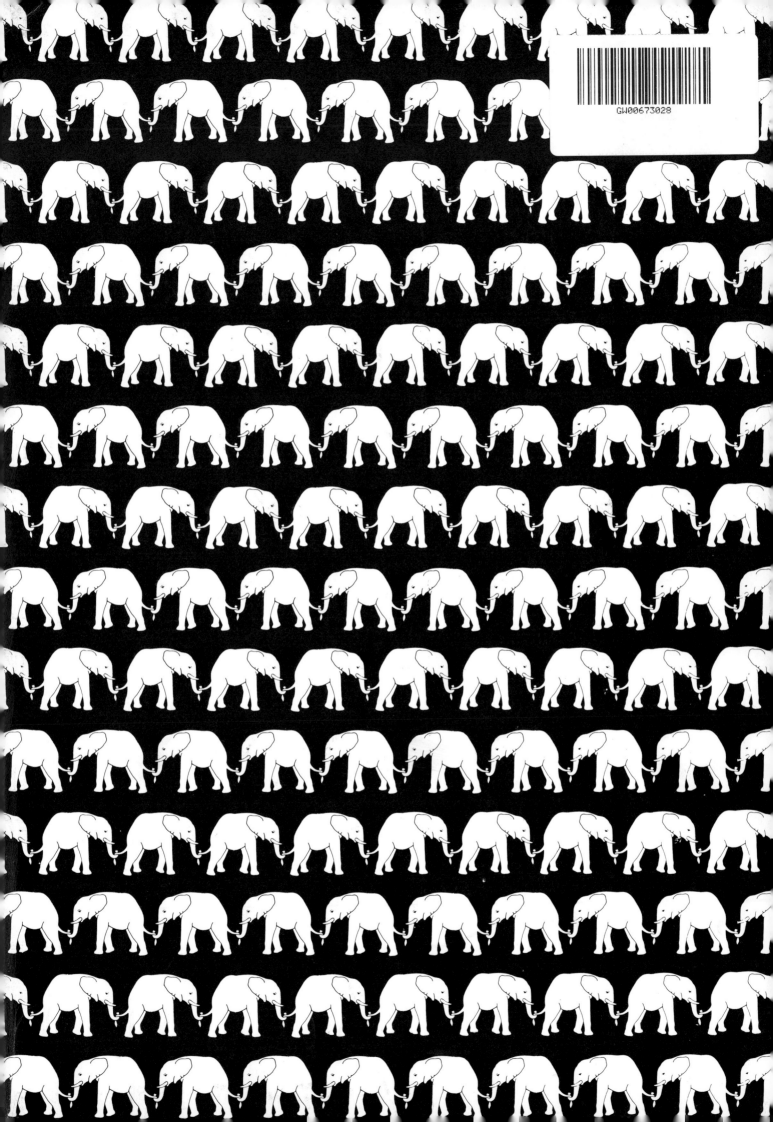

THE WHITE ELEPHANT CELEBRITY COOKBOOK

THE WHITE
ELEPHANT
CELEBRITY
COOKBOOK

**WEIDENFELD
& NICOLSON**

This book, the second edition,
is dedicated to my two children,
Cookie and Paul,
and to the memory of their father,
Victor, to whom the three of us
owe so much.

PREFACE

THE VICTOR BRUSA MEMORIAL FUND FOR CHILDREN

This year, 1979, has been declared the *Year of The Child*, so it is timely that the second edition of the White Elephant Cook Book should appear for the year's end. This *Year of The Child* has been treated internationally, but I must be truthful and say that working as we do with the Membership of our two London clubs, we have to restrict ourselves to the children without hope within our own limited boundaries of this country. What we manage to do with the help of our Members all over the world and of every nationality, is to send on holiday children from all parts of this country and of every race, colour and religion through the N.S.P.C.C. Children whose only ailment is lack of care, love and attention. In recent years we have extended our Fund to incorporate Battered Families, that horrible phrase which has now become part of our language, and sadly, part of daily lives.

It is perhaps difficult for those of us who hope we do our best for our children, to realise the full horror of this social ignominy. It is almost impossible for the problem to be solved with money. But money helps. We have found that by sending children, and sometimes families on holiday under supervision, free from the cares and pressures of their abnormally miserable lives, that they have a brief chance to become real parents and children for albeit too short a time. Sometimes this brief restoration to life as it should be, causes a realisation of what has happened and the chances of battering again, through pressures, reduce.

There is the incredible case of a child who had been thought to be suffering from polio. A school lent its premises and some of its staff for about fifty children one year. The school had a heated swimming pool. An N.S.P.C.C. welfare officer and some of the teachers lifted the small girl out of her wheelchair and floated her into the water. Within a few minutes the child was swimming alone and unaided. She swam to the edge of the pool and climbed up the steps and walked towards an astounded group of children and grown-ups unable to believe their eyes. The child did not have polio at all. She had been slow to walk and had been treated as a cripple. That was a kind of miracle. There have been many cases of children unable to speak to strangers for fear of being hit, starting their holidays sullen and quiet, and returning two weeks later smiling and laughing.

The Fund has been called the *VICTOR BRUSA MEMORIAL FUND FOR CHILDREN* after the father of my two, now grown up, extremely privileged children. He died in 1965, five years after we had opened the White Elephant in Curzon Street. He knew poverty and hardship as a child, and was determined that one day he would try to do whatever he could to help under-privileged children. We have tried hard to carry out what he wanted. The sale of this book will help towards one child going on holiday – a tiny drop in the ocean. But we do collect money and receive many contributions all the year round from many of our kind members. Years in which we do not have a book to boost the fund.

Since the first edition some of the contributors have died, but as a tribute to them we have decided to leave the recipes and art work of Peter Finch, Geraldo, Laurence Harvey, Jack Hawkins and Vicky.

By adding some new names to this second edition, people and graphic artists, in particular, have been generous beyond words. Arnold Schwartzman and Sue Rogers have again brought together more distinguished illustrators and photographers and given them a free hand to choose their own celebrity to interpret both them and their recipes as they wanted. Some of the pictures may startle you and some of the cooks involved but I think you will agree that they have earned their fun and worked without a penny to help give under-privileged children a chance in life. Maybe only one chance, but at least that.

Stella Richman

ACKNOWLEDGEMENTS
& THANKS

To all the celebrities who contributed their favourite recipes and whom we drove mad getting them.

To all the designers, illustrators and photographers who gave not only their time but all the materials necessary, and who have given us the original art work to raise extra money for the Children's Fund.

To Chris and Eric at the WHITE ELEPHANT, Chef and Patissier respectively, who so lovingly cooked many of the recipes for the art work.

To the typographer, Roger Baker of Face Photosetting and John Gorham for designing the cover.

To Christopher Falkus and Richard Hussey at Weidenfeld & Nicolson.

To Arnold Schwartzman, the Design Editor and co-ordinator whose persistance and creativity has won us so many beautiful art contributions and awards.

To Sue Rogers, my assistant and friend, without whom there would be no book at all.

And to all our members and their friends who have bought copies of the book.

STARTERS

MAIN DISHES

PUDDINGS & CAKES

BITS & PIECES

STELLA RICHMAN

There are more restaurant stories than I have had hot dinners, and over nineteen years of the White Elephant, Curzon Street and seven years of the White Elephant on the River, I have eaten a great number. When I'm looking a little off colour or troubled, any waiter serving me restaurants fills my plate up to the brim since to all Italians, filling the stomach is probably considered the best way to overcome worries. I have eaten my way through more bread and butter puddings, rice puddings, and pasta, than anyone else currently living. Our English Patisserie Chef, Eric, will not only be my downfall but the downfall of many distinguished members with his beautiful sweet trolley. I have never known our Chef at the White Elephant, Chris, another Englishman, fail us when someone asks for something not on the menu, and any weight I have put on has been entirely due to the dedication of these two marvellously creative people.

Coming up to our twentieth year, it has been the greatest source of pleasure that at least five of the restaurant staff have been with me the whole of that time, and this is as good a time as any to thank my two Managers, Rinaldo at the White Elephant, Domenico at the White Elephant on the River, our two senior Barmen, Orlando and Nino, and Giovanni our Malvolio-like wine waiter at the White Elephant; together with others who

have been here for about thirteen years like Marc, Jorge, Marino, Erasmo, Donato and Piero, who all seem to me an extension of my family. In some of the difficult years they have stood by me through thick and thin, fat and lean. Without their friendship and support there would not be one White Elephant in London, let alone two.

I'm hoping that as we come up to twenty years together, we can continue into the next twenty when the first grandchildren should start to appear, just as we have been children of members come into the restaurants and they are now delightful young men and women. Those children who now enjoy throwing ice-cream at the waiters at the White Elephant on the River Sunday Brunch, will perhaps be bringing in their children to do the same thing in the next two decades.

To all our Members who have supported us from the beginning, we send our good wishes, and my own personal thanks to those who have helped to keep our Children's Fund going. We are the lucky ones to whom one hot dinner more or less means very little.

Silvano, who used to be one of our Head Waiters and is now the Maitre D at the Leonardo da Vinci in Rome, created the following dish. It is a lovely and painless way of becoming a little high without drinking.

Rigatoni Silvano

Serves 4

butter
large handful of bacon bits
4 drops Tabasco
vodka (according to taste and capacity)
1 small can peeled tomatoes
1½ packets Rigatoni (approximately 1½ lb)
grated Parmesan cheese
single cream

Put some butter and pieces of bacon in a frying pan on a low heat.

Make sure the bacon is well done.

Add 4 drops of Tabasco.

Flame with a double vodka (if you're using it for a party starter—double the quantity of vodka).

Add can of peeled tomatoes.

Throw in the pre-cooked Rigatoni, and turn it over several times.

Add some Parmesan cheese and cream, turning slowly all the time.

The ingredients, not you.

Serve piping hot with more grated cheese.

That's it.

It's amazing what a little vodka can do to this standard Italian dish.

Stella Richman

SHELLEY WINTERS

Caesar Salad

Serves 4

1 *clove garlic*
½ *cup* olive oil*
1 *cup* cubed French bread or ready-made croûtons*
1½ *teaspoons salt*
¼ *teaspoon dry or hot mustard*
freshly ground black pepper
5 *anchovy fillets*
few drops Worcester sauce
3 *tablespoons wine vinegar*
1 *raw egg*
juice of 1 *lemon*
2 *heads cos lettuce*
2–3 *tablespoons grated Parmesan cheese*

Peel and slice garlic.
Soak olive oil with the garlic for 24 hours.
Sauté the cubed French bread in 2 tablespoons of the oil.
Into a large salad bowl place salt, mustard, pepper, anchovy, Worcester sauce, wine vinegar, and remaining olive oil.
Blend with a fork.
Now add the egg and lemon juice, and mix well.
Break the lettuce into a bowl.
Toss well with the dressing.
Add the cheese and croûtons before serving.
Toss all well.
Serve with grilled steak as a first course.

I first tasted this in Mexico when I was attending a bullfight with Tony Quinn.

*1 *cup* = 8 *fl oz*

"I first tasted this in Mexico when I was attending a bullfight with Tony Quinn"

SHELLEY WINTERS

Peter Blake. 1973.

PICKLED HERRING   ILLUSTRATOR: JOHN GORHAM

ARNOLD SCHWARTZMAN

Pickled Herring

It is terribly important that it is understood that this is a two day operation.

Gut 6 (or however many you wish) herring, removing their heads and tails too. Place in an oven-proof casserole. Add 1 bay leaf, 10 black peppercorns, and a pinch of salt to taste, plus 4 medium sliced onions. Cover the herring with wine or malt vinegar. Put the lid on the casserole and cook in a very, very slow oven for 2 hours (225°F, gas $\frac{1}{4}$). Remove from the oven and when cold, place in the refrigerator.

The following morning taste and see whether you think more vinegar should be added. Serve with brown bread and butter.

LEE REMICK

Here's my recipe for the simplest and tastiest Gaspacho ever.

Gaspacho

Serves 8

1 *clove garlic, peeled and chopped*
1 *medium-sized onion, chopped*
1 *cucumber, chopped*
3 *ripe tomatoes, peeled and chopped (or*
1 *tin)*
$\frac{1}{4}$ *cup* vinegar*
$\frac{3}{4}$ *cup* tomato juice*
good dash salt
good dash cayenne
$\frac{1}{4}$ *cup* olive oil*
4 *eggs, well beaten*
salt and pepper to taste

Combine the vegetables with all the ingredients, except the eggs, and purée in the blender.
Mix in the well beaten eggs.
Season to taste.
Chill.
Serve with the following garnishes, each in a separate bowl: croûtons, diced cucumber, chopped scallions, chopped green pepper, chopped ripe tomato.
*1 *cup* = 8 *fl oz*

Enjoy!

Lee Remick

LEE REMICK   PHOTOGRAPHER: DONALD McCULLIN

MILLICENT MARTIN   ILLUSTRATOR: DICK SMITH

MILLICENT MARTIN

Smoked Salmon Dip

Serves 8

½ lb smoked salmon ends
½ lb cream cheese
½ pt double cream
lemon juice
paprika
pepper to taste
lumpfish or salmon caviar

Blend salmon and cream cheese until purée.

Add cream until a dip consistency is achieved.

Add lemon juice, paprika and pepper to taste.

Arrange in a bowl and cover with lumpfish or caviar.

Serve with crackers.

Chicken Watercress

Serves 4

1 3 lb chicken (or 8 pieces)
1 oz butter
1 tablespoon oil
6 oz onions (sliced)
1 large bunch watercress
3 oz chickpeas
6 fl oz chicken stock
4 tablespoons sour cream
fresh ground pepper to flavour

Brown chicken in butter and oil until the skin is crisp.

Remove and place in a casserole.

Add onion to fat and fry until soft.

Clean watercress and add to onion and cook for 2 minutes.

Add chickpeas to chicken and cover with onions and watercress.

Pour over stock and season with ground pepper.

Cover and cook in the oven (350°F, gas 4) for about an hour.

Remove chicken and keep warm.

Purée the remaining sauce in a blender and add sour cream; replace chicken in casserole and pour purée over it.

Serve with wild rice.

Both these recipes taste great!

MAXINE AUDLEY

Watercress 'Etcetera' Soup

This soup can be served hot or cold.

½ small chopped onion or 1 small leek
knob of butter
1 beef or chicken cube dissolved in ¾ pint
water
2 bunches watercress
2 carrots
1 small turnip
2 sticks celery
moderate quantity chopped parsley
moderate quantity chopped endives
fresh cream and/or beaten yolk of egg (if
both cream and egg are used, the soup is
extra delicious)
salt and pepper

Fry the onion or leek gently in the butter until soft, but not browned.

At the same time, mix the beef or chicken cube in hot water.

Put both into a largish saucepan.

Add all the chopped vegetables, saving a few watercress leaves for decoration.

Bring to the boil, and simmer gently for 5–10 minutes.

Pour all into the liquidizer (if available), and liquidize for 1 minute, then return to the saucepan and simmer for another 5 minutes.

Reduce the heat to minimum, and add cream and/or egg yolk just before serving.

It is important that the soup should be just hot, but not boiling or bubbling when the cream and egg yolk are added; then, naturally, stir well with a wooden spoon.

For those who do not own a liquidizer, this soup is equally delicious if the ingredients are cooked a little longer, and then put through a sieve.

If it is to be served cold, a little more cream should be added when the soup has cooled, and before putting the whole dish in the fridge.

Also, the ingredients are variable. For example, leave out the turnip or leek, and substitute lettuce or frozen peas; alternatively, peeled tomatoes or tomato juice can be added, although tomato tends to overpower the rest unless used sparingly.

Oh! I forgot to mention salt and pepper to taste!

A Special Salad

2 hardboiled egg yolks
2 sieved boiled potatoes
½ small chopped onion
1 teaspoon mustard (preferably Dijon)
4 tablespoons olive oil
2 tablespoons wine vinegar
soupçon anchovy sauce (to taste)
salt and pepper (to taste)

Mix all the ingredients together in a wooden bowl, then add the lettuce, endive, chicory, tomatoes, raw carrots, watercress, green pepper, raw cab-bage, or any combination of raw salad or vegetable that may be desired, and stir the whole lot together.

Maxine Audley

Watercress,

etc,
APPLO

etc,
CUPID

etc,
TEMPO HEAVY CONDENSED

etc,
PLUTO

etc,
ELIZABETH ROMAN

etc,
HERKULES

etc,
HEMLOCK

etc,
ARNOLD BOLD

etc,
CRAW CLARENDON CONDENSED

etc,
KOLOSS CONDENSED

etc,
ITALIAN OLD STYLE

etc,
GERMAN TITLE

etc,
BLANCHARD SOLID

etc,
FUTURA BOOK

etc,
COOPER BLACK ITALIC

etc,
TROOPER ROMAN

etc,
PLAYBILL

etc,
ALFER ETA

soup.

WATERCRESS ETC. SOUP   DESIGN FACE PHOTOSETTING

WENDY CRAIG

Stuffed Courgettes

Serves 4

1 *large onion, finely chopped*
2 *oz butter*
6 *rashers streaky bacon, chopped*
¼ *lb mushrooms, chopped*
4 *large tomatoes, peeled and chopped*
good pinch mixed herbs
½ *clove garlic, crushed*
salt and pepper
2 *small courgettes per person, or 1 large*

Fry onion in 1 oz butter, then fry the bacon; drain on greaseproof paper.

Fry the mushrooms in the remaining butter until soft, then add the tomatoes, herbs, garlic, and seasoning.
Cook for a further 3–4 minutes.
Drain off any excess fat, and add the onion and bacon.
Cut a wide wedge in the top of each courgette, lengthwise that is, and lay them in an oven-proof dish.
Fill the wedges with the mixture, cover with cooking foil and cook in a moderate oven (350 °F, gas 4) for between 30–40 minutes.

Blackberry Fool

Serves 6

1 *tin blackberries*
1 *large carton double cream*
caster sugar, to taste
angelica

Put the blackberries and about half of the juice through a fine sieve, saving a few firm berries.
Whip the cream until it's quite thick, then add the blackberry purée and sugar, folding gently.
Pour into a glass dish, and chill for 4–5 hours.
Decorate with angelica and one or two firm blackberries you've saved.

Ginger Delights

Serves 4

1 *small tin pineapple pieces*
2 *pieces stem ginger*
¼ *pint double cream*
1 *tablespoon caster sugar*
1 *packet ginger biscuits*

Pour the juice off the pineapple, and reserve it.
Cut the pineapple pieces in half, and chop the stem ginger into tiny morsels.
Whip the cream, and add to it the sugar, ginger, and pineapple.

Soak the ginger biscuits in the juice you've kept, and arrange around the sides of individual serving dishes.
Spoon the cream mixture into them and allow to chill for about 12 hours.
Decorate with a piece of stem ginger.

Happy munching!

FRESH ASPARAGUS   ILLUSTRATOR: LAURENCE KLONARIS

JOE LOSS

Fresh Asparagus

At the end of May and beginning of June, home-grown asparagus appears in the shops in England.

The season only lasts a few weeks although imported asparagus can be bought expensively for the rest of the year.

Serves 4

Take 2 lb of asparagus and gently scrape the lower parts of the stems.

Tie it in bundles of 10–12.

Bring a large saucepan of lightly salted boiling water to the boil and place the bundles of asparagus upright in it, leaving the tips above the water.

The asparagus is cooked when the tips look soft.

Drain carefully and try not to damage the tips.

Serve on individual plates with warm melted butter.

They taste best eaten with your fingers!

OLIVER REED

Prawns Mergertated in Sherry

Serves 4

24 *raw Dublin Bay prawns*
4 *oz butter*
salt and pepper
8 *fluid oz medium-dry sherry*
8 *fluid oz cream*
3 *egg yolks*
chili powder
parsley
2 *cups rice*
2 *cups cold water*
¼ *teaspoon salt*
1 *teaspoon oil*

First drink several large glasses of sherry!

Fry the prawns in butter, seasoning with salt and pepper.

Add the sherry, and boil to reduce.

Remove from heat, and add the cream and yolks, stirring all the time.

Return to a very low heat until thickened.

Finish off the sherry yourself!

A little chili powder and parsley may be dusted over the top for a spicy flavour and colour, if desired.

Meanwhile wash the rice.

Add water and salt.

Bring to the boil and cover with lid.

Turn the heat very low for about 20 minutes.

A teaspoon of oil may be added.

Then serve, preferably with at least another bottle of sherry for each person, so that if it's a disaster you'll be too drunk to notice.

Curried Chicken Knockers

Serves 4

2 *bay leaves*
1 *clove garlic*
2 *cloves*
2 *oz butter*
6 *plump chicken breasts*
2 *onions, chopped*
2 *teaspoons curry powder*
1 *teaspoon chili powder*
1 *green pepper, sliced*
½ *level teaspoon powdered turmeric*
¼ *level teaspoon ginger*
½ *lb tomatoes*
½ *pint chicken stock*
tomato purée
1 *tablespoon desiccated coconut*
4 *fluid oz yoghurt*
salt and pepper

Fry the bay leaves, garlic, and cloves in butter for 1½ minutes.

Add the chicken breasts, brown slightly, remove, and keep warm.

Add the chopped onions, and fry until transparent.

Add curry powder and chilli powder.

Return the chicken, add sliced green pepper, turmeric, ginger, and tomatoes.

Add stock, tomato purée, and stir.

Bring to the boil adding coconut and yoghurt.

Lower heat, add salt and pepper to taste and simmer for 1½ hours.

Add more stock if necessary.

Serve with rice, a side dish of cucumber, chopped onions, yoghurt, with green chilis . . . raw for the brave.

OLIVER REED   ILLUSTRATOR: JEAN MULATIER

AVOCADOS GUACAMOLE   ILLUSTRATOR: MICHAEL ENGLISH

VINCENT PRICE

Guacamole

2 *avocado pears*
3 *tablespoons lemon juice*
1 *small grated onion*
1 *small green chilli, chopped*
$\frac{1}{8}$ *teaspoon ground coriander*
$\frac{1}{2}$ *clove garlic, mashed*
salt
3 *tablespoons mayonnaise*
chopped, seeded, and peeled tomato (about
3 *small ones)*
dash of cayenne or Tabasco

Peel and seed the avocados, but *make sure that you save the seeds.*

Mash the flesh either smooth or slightly lumpy (I prefer lumpy).

Add the rest of the ingredients, mix well, then put the seeds on top.

This prevents discolouration.

Chill, but remove seeds a little before serving.

Serve before dinner with drinks, crisps or biscuits, or a great glop on top of shredded lettuce as a salad with dinner.

Avocado is also delicious with sautéed calves' liver—just make rings of it, sprinkle with lemon, dust with seasoned flour, and sauté with the liver.

Raw mushroom and avocado salad is great with anything—add an oil, vinegar, mustard, garlic dressing with a little sugar.

(Basically most of these recipes come from our cookbook *A Treasury of Great Recipes*, in its fifth printing and still going strong.)

Since the advent of the avocado into England, I've found rather limited use of this delicious fruit, served mostly *vinagrette* or stuffed with prawns etc.

In California via Mexico we use the riper avocados to make the all purpose Guacamole.

Vincent Price

ERIC SYKES

Gambas au Gratin

Serves 4

1 *clove garlic*
$\frac{1}{2}$ *pint shelled prawns*
4 *tomatoes, skinned and sliced*
2 *hardboiled eggs, sliced*
$\frac{1}{2}$ *pint cheese sauce*

Grease an oven-proof dish, and rub well with garlic.

Arrange the prawns, tomatoes, and eggs in layers in the dish, and pour over the cheese sauce.

Bake in the oven (350 °F, gas 3) for 10 minutes.

Serve piping hot, and while they're eating it, slip out and have some egg and chips.

Egg & Chips

Break the shells of 2 eggs and allow the contents to hit the pan.

Nip down to the chip shop, and return with a hot ten-pennyworth; bung the lot on a plate—then slip out and have sausage and mash.

Sausage & Mash

Take 2 lb of sausages—etc.

ERIC SYKES   ILLUSTRATOR: PAULINE ELLISON

ERNIE WISE/FRENCH ONION SOUP   ILLUSTRATOR: ALAN MANHAM

ERNIE WISE

Liver Pâté

Serves 4–6

8–12 *oz lamb or chicken liver*
4 *oz fat bacon*
1 *oz butter*
1 *oz flour*
¼ *pint milk*
½ *teaspoon mixed herbs, if liked*
1 *egg*
2 *teaspoons grated onion*
2 *teaspoons sherry or brandy*
1 *teaspoon salt and pepper*

Wash liver and remove sinews.
Mince finely with the bacon.

Make thick sauce of butter, flour, and milk, stirring well.

Add seasoning to taste.

Mix well the liver, bacon, and sauce.

Add the beaten egg, grated onion, sherry, salt and pepper.

Place mixture in a greased oven-proof dish.

Place this in a tin filled with water about 1 inch deep.

Cover with foil or grease-proof paper and cook in the oven (350°F, gas 4) for 1 hour, until firm.

French Onion Soup

Serves 4

4 *medium-sized onions*
butter
little sugar
1½ *pints water with 1 stock cube*
1 *small bottle white wine*
4 *oz grated Gruyère cheese*
toast
salt and pepper

Fry the sliced onions slowly in butter but do not let them brown.

When well cooked sprinkle with sugar.

Place in a pan with water and meat cube or stock.

Bring to the boil and simmer for 20 minutes.

Reduce the heat to a gentle simmer, and add white wine.

Cook for 10 minutes.

Divide the cheese into 4 on pieces of toast 1½ inches square, and put into soup bowls.

Fill with soup, and place under the grill until cheese is golden-brown.

Add salt and pepper to taste.

If you make a large amount of this soup, it keeps very well in a deep freeze.

I do like my wife's Liver Pâté and her French Onion Soup but the only trouble is that I find it very filling, and am unable to eat the rest of the meal.

You may not believe this but I was a cook in the Merchant Navy in the war.

I still enjoy cooking to this day, and with all the exciting dishes there are like 'Chicken Take Away' and that chicken 'that's finger licken good', I still prefer bacon and eggs.

TED KOTCHEFF

Bop (Bulgarian Bean Soup)

2 cups white haricot beans
4 pints cold water
1 cup coarsely chopped onions
4 fresh coarsely chopped tomatoes (or 1 small tin tomatoes)
7 tablespoons olive oil
2 teaspoons paprika
2 teaspoons fresh or dried mint (garnish)
salt and pepper to taste

Spread out beans on the table and remove any stones or grit, wash well.

Cover the beans with cold water and place on heat.

Add onion, tomatoes, olive oil, paprika, and pepper.

Bring to the boil and then simmer until beans are soft.

The time for this varies according to the beans used but is usually around $2\frac{1}{2}$ hours.

Now add salt and simmer for another 20 minutes.

Always add the salt when the beans are almost cooked, never before because salt hardens the beans.

Beans may be soaked in water for a few hours for quicker cooking.

The amount of water you cook the beans in can vary according to the texture desired at the end.

More water makes the dish a soup.

Less water and the dish is more like a stew.

This is one of the most famous of Bulgarian peasant dishes; tasty, filling, and economical to make. Bop is a soup and may be used as an opening course, but because it is so satisfying, in Bulgaria it is often eaten as the main dish, accompanied by plenty of brown bread and butter and a mixed salad.

Ted Kotcheff

BOP BEAN SOUP   ILLUSTRATOR: LESLIE CHAPMAN

'FISH-PORTER'   PHOTOGRAPHER: ROB GAGE

THEA PORTER

Pancakes Stuffed with Fish

pancake batter
fat for frying, olive oil
1 large white fish (bass, cod, or similar)
½ pint Béchamel sauce, made with 1 onion,
chopped parsley, white wine, and lemon
juice
cream
Parmesan cheese
black pepper, salt

Make thin pancakes—I always find these easier if batter is made the day before and put in the refrigerator.

Clean, wash, and salt the fish, then wrap in a newspaper soaked in olive oil and lemon juice.

Bake in a moderate oven (350 °F, gas 4) till tender and flaky—about 30 minutes.

Flake, salt, and fold in Béchamel sauce.

Roll the mixture into the pancakes, and arrange in a large oven-proof dish.

Cover with cream and Parmesan cheese.

Add a little black pepper, and heat gently in a slow oven (250 °F, gas ½) for 20 minutes.

Brown quickly under a hot grill, and serve.

I have many favourite dishes that are all connected with people and places, and that remind me of large, leisured, sumptuous meals in France or the Lebanon.

This is a dish I first had at a very bourgeois old-style house in Beirut.

One of those old houses with cool, marble floors, high vaulted ceilings and precious carpets hanging on the walls surrounding the Lebanese equivalent of the Stag at Bay: a large sepia photograph of some grand ancestor in official Turkish garb at the end of the Ottoman Empire.

The pancakes were handed round by a 14 year old servant as the delicate, fattening start to a long meal.

Thea Porter

JOHN CAVANAGH

Double Favourite

Serves 4

shredded lettuce
4 oz smoked salmon, cut into thin strips
4 oz white crab meat

For sauce, mix the following ingredients:

2 tablespoons mayonnaise
2 tablespoons whipped cream
1 teaspoon French mustard
1 dessertspoon grapefruit
juice, unsweetened
dash of Worcester sauce
lemon juice and tomato ketchup to taste

Place shredded lettuce into sundae dishes. Add alternately in layers the smoked salmon, crab meat and sauce finishing with smoked salmon and sauce on top.

JANET SUZMAN

Boula

Here goes for a recipe of great originality!

My mother, to whom I owe practically *everything*, gave me this.

So to her, with love—

Serves 20

4–5 *cans pea soup*
4 *cans turtle soup*
$\frac{1}{4}$ *teaspoon cayenne pepper*
pinch of mace
2 *cloves grated garlic*
1 *cup cream*
salt
1 *cup sherry*

Mix all the ingredients together.

Serve cold with whipped cream and Parmesan cheese on top, or sprinkle with paprika.

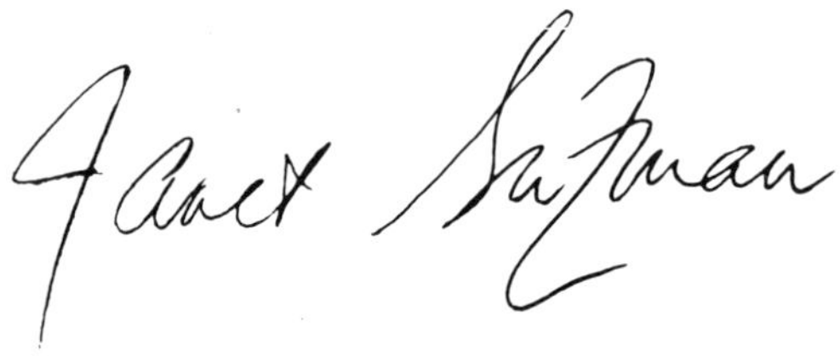

Janet Suzman

TURTLE & PEA SOUP   ILLUSTRATOR: BRIAN GRIMWOOD

MARIANNE & PETER NOBLE

Cheese & Cucumber Mousse

Serves 6

1 large cucumber
salt and white pepper
6 oz demi-sel cheese
1 teaspoon onion juice
¼ pint boiling water or chicken stock
1 level tablespoon gelatine soaked in 3 tablespoons cold water
1 tablespoon caster sugar
2 tablespoons white wine vinegar
pinch of mace or coriander
½ pint double cream
watercress to garnish

Dice the cucumber, sprinkle with salt, and leave pressed and weighted for 30 minutes to remove excess juice.

Work the cheese with onion juice and seasoning.

Pour water or stock on to the soaked gelatine, stir until dissolved, and add to cheese.

Drain the cucumber thoroughly and mix with sugar, vinegar, and spice.

When the cheese mixture is quite cold, fold in cucumber and lightly whipped cream.

Pour into an oiled ring mould and leave to set.

Turn out the mousse when refrigerated, and fill the centre with well-washed watercress.

Serve with brown bread and butter.

— Peter & Marianne Noble —

TIM RICE
Kathleen's Cauliflower Soup

Serves 4

1 *fully grown cauliflower*
¾ *pint chicken stock*
2 *oz butter*
1 *oz plain flour*
seasoning (that's salt, pepper, etc.)
grated cheese

The cauliflower should be mature, not too hefty and a medium size will do.

Simmer the said vegetable in enough water leaving on all the stalk and the crisp green outer leaves.

When cooked (this is up to you to judge, could be a mere 3 minutes with a garden-fresh specimen, but a lot longer with a more elderly plant) liquidize it.

Then melt the butter in a pan and stir in the flour to make a roux. (A roux is what you get when you stir melted butter with flour.)

Stir in a generous quantity of grated cheese.

Add the chicken stock gradually and bring the whole shooting match to the boil.

Now add the liquid cauliflower and cook for just a few minutes more.

This never goes wrong when Kathleen does it and has a good chance of working well when others do it.

Some connoisseurs like to add more grated cheese or even double cream (a dash) to the finished creation.

Sling in the seasoning at more or less any stage as you feel fit.

This one will run and run.

Tim Rice

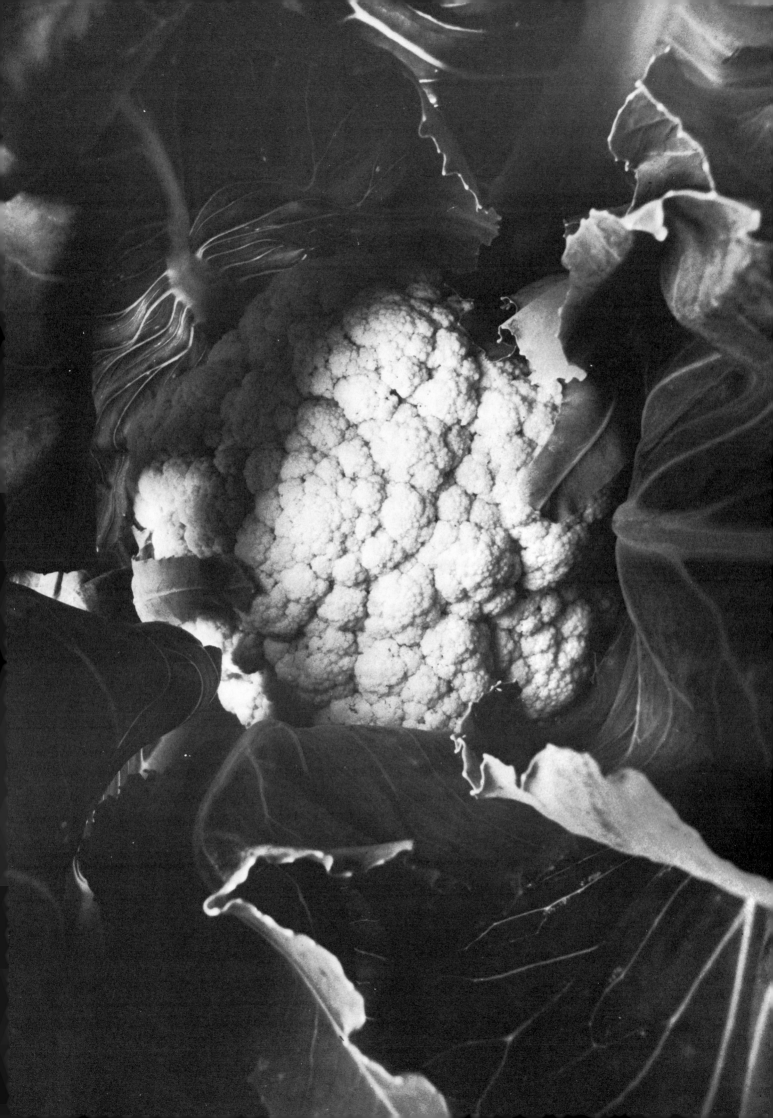

JOHN SCHLESINGER

Kebabs

Have Garam Masala prepared and ready (see second recipe).

Serve with boiled rice.

½ lb very lean, finely minced meat (lamb may be best)
1 teaspoon mustard seeds
1 teaspoon poppy seeds
1½ dessertspoons lentils
pinch of dry ginger
2 cloves garlic
1 teaspoon cumin
1 egg
salt and pepper
chili
fresh cream
finely chopped mint
whipped egg white
oil for frying

Put the meat and spices in a heavy pan, cover with water, and boil for 30 minutes, till about the consistency of mashed potato.

Allow to cool, then pulverize with a pestle and mortar or in an electric blender.

Now add 1 teaspoon Garam Masala (see below) mixed with egg, salt, pepper, and chili.

Make sure that all the excess moisture has been drained off.

Roll into balls, and fashion these into cups.

Into each cup put cream and mint (or finely chopped onions with a little lemon juice).

Roll the cups carefully into balls again, so that the cream and mint mixture is in the centre.

Dip in the beaten egg white, and fry in hot oil.

Garam Masala

1 tablespoon coriander
1 tablespoon cumin
1 teaspoon black pepper
1 teaspoon cloves
few sticks cinnamon
6 large black cardamom seeds
6 white cardamom
4 dried bay leaves

Roast for 1 minute in a hot oven, and grind.

Keep in a sealed jar for all basic Indian cooking.

This is a recipe for Kebabs that I learned in Sikkim when I was staying there recently on a trip through India and the Far East to get away from films for a while.

It is a good recipe for appetizers, though it could be served as a main course.

JOHN SCHLESINGER/INDIAN KEBABS   ILLUSTRATOR: DAVID POCKNELL

REGGIE ROSE   DESIGN : ARNOLD SCHWARTZMAN, PHOTOGRAPHER : PETER HOWE

REGINALD ROSE

This beautiful creation used to be sneaked out of Crazy Sheldon's house in a greasy brown paper bag while his grandmother was screaming over the telephone at the poultryman about the washed-out colour of his chicken fat, and eaten by our group in a vacant lot with bare hands because Crazy Sheldon always forgot the rye bread.

The biggest kid, not Crazy Sheldon and certainly not I, but a great hulk named Enzo Riccardelli who swore he was Jewish (his exact words on that subject were: 'I'll kill the first creep who says I ain't a mockie!') got to turn the paper bag inside out and lick it clean.

I personally paid Crazy Sheldon nine cents to stand at his grandmother's side one day and write down this recipe step by step as 'those golden hands coaxed it together.

I pass it on to you with a warning.

Should you, while taking the finished product over to the Vicarage for tea, run into anyone named Enzo Riccardelli, approximately seven feet tall, with a jagged scar running from the corner of his left eye down to his belly button, let him have as much of it as he wants.

I guarantee he's Jewish.

It's merely chopped liver but, properly made, it can make you lie down and die happy.

Chopped Chicken Liver à la Crazy Sheldon who used to live around the corner when I was a kid's grandmother

5 *medium-sized onions*
6 *tablespoons rendered chicken fat (or salad oil)*
1 *lb fresh chicken livers*
4 *hardboiled eggs*
1 *heel (or slice) rye bread*
sugar
powdered nutmeg
4 *oz sour cream*
salt and freshly ground pepper

Chop 3 onions, and sauté in a large frying pan in 4 tablespoons of the rendered chicken fat (or salad oil) until they are just golden-brown.

Add chicken livers and sauté with the onions until cooked, but not dry.

Mince sautéed livers and onions, along with the pan juices.

Also mince remaining raw onions, hardboiled eggs and heel of rye bread.

You now have a bowl full of minced everything which you attack with a fork, mixing it all thoroughly together while adding the remaining chicken fat.

Add a generous pinch of sugar, and a small pinch of powdered nutmeg.

Then add cream, and keep mixing.

Don't get discouraged.

There's nothing good on television anyway.

Season to taste.

It will require more salt than you think.

Keep mixing with the fork until the consistency is to your liking.

If it seems too dry, add a bit more fat: refrigerate gradually.

When it is cool, but not chilled, lock yourself in your bedroom and eat the whole thing, as it is, or spread on rye bread or black bread.

To hell with the Vicar's tea!

Reggie

GALIA & CHAIM TOPOL

Gefilte Fish

Serves 8–10

6 *onions*
1 *carp*
4 *hardboiled eggs*
salt and pepper
4 *raw eggs*
2 *tablespoons sugar*
martemelle flour, if necessary
4 *sticks celery*
parsley
slices of carrot } *to taste*
water

Boil 3 onions slightly, to take away the bitterness.

Take the fish from bones, and mince the carp.

Separately, mince the onions that have been slightly boiled.

Mince the hardboiled eggs, and then bind these ingredients together.

Season to taste, then add the raw eggs and sugar.

Roll this mixture into balls, and if too soft add a little martemelle flour.

Slice the remaining onions into a large pan with the celery, parsley, and slices of carrot.

Cover with water, and bring to the boil.

Place the fish balls on top making sure that the water is just covering them.

Cover and bring to a steady boil on a moderate heat.

Leave for $1–1\frac{1}{2}$ hours.

Remove lid, and wait until the fish is cold before putting it onto a serving dish, otherwise it will break.

Serve cold.

This is a delicious Polish recipe and a favourite of ours.

GALIA & CHAIM
Topol

56

TOPOL   ILLUSTRATOR: SIMMS TABACK

NORMAN ROSSINGTON   PHOTOGRAPHER: GORDON MOORE

NORMAN ROSSINGTON

Mushrooms Rossington

Serves 4

1 *lb mushrooms*
½ *cup olive oil*
salt and pepper
1 *teaspoon thyme*
mixed herbs
2–3 *glasses wine (or more!)*

Wipe the mushrooms, but don't peel them—a waste of money!

Sauté in oil in a heavy pan with lid, on a fairly high heat until brown.

Add all the seasoning.

Mix together, and continue cooking.

Turn up the flame to maximum, and after about 1 minute add wine and let it reduce until there's just a little sauce.

Can be eaten cold as an hors d'oeuvre or hot with steak or chops.

Norman Rossington

CLEO LAINE &
JOHN DANKWORTH

Potato Pancake

$\frac{1}{2}$ *lb potatoes*
1 *medium-sized onion*
salt
$\frac{1}{4}$ *lb flour*
1 *egg*
lard for frying

Coarsely grate the raw potatoes and onion, add salt and flour, then the beaten egg to make a batter of dropping consistency.

Heat some lard in a frying pan, and add the mixture, spreading it like a pancake.

Fry rather slowly on both sides, and serve immediately it is cooked.

MAIN DISHES

MAX BYGRAVES

Scampi Walewska

Serves 4

1 lb scampi
little white wine or fish stock
salt and pepper
1 pint Béchamel sauce
4 oz grated Parmesan cheese
4 oz cooked lobster
4 slices truffle (if available)

Poach the scampi in a very small amount of white wine or fish stock, seasoned and covered with grease-proof paper.

Prepare Béchamel sauce, and add 3 oz of the grated cheese.

Remove scampi from the cooking liquor and place in an earthenware serving dish.

Arrange into 4 separate portions.

Place a slice of lobster on each portion, coat with the sauce, and sprinkle the top with the remaining cheese.

Put a slice of truffle on top, and brown the dish under a hot grill.

The cooking liquor may be added to the sauce.

A well chilled bottle of Piesporter is my idea of a fine wine with it—expensive but good.

Vichysoisse cold for starters, and, I know it's the wrong way round, but I like it, a good juicy melon for dessert —um, lovely!

If you are thinking of doing it tonight, give me a ring, I'll come and join you.

My address: C/o Hospital for Tropical Diseases, Gray's Inn Road, London, WC2.

But back to the White Elephant, if you are the customer—the Golden Goose, if you are the owner.

The first time I experienced Scampi Walewska was at the White Elephant— I had just sold my house, and was able to afford a table for two.

We had sacked the cook—a lady from Spain—whom I had christened 'Helen of Troy' because every meal she served was 'swimming in Grease'.
She was the only person I know who could burn water—mind you, she called it soup.

Since she left us, she went to work for a well-known T.V. personality.

You can judge how he rates her cooking—four nights a week he eats at the studio canteen, the rest of the week he spends at the Hospital for Tropical Diseases in Gray's Inn Road.

CHARLES AZNAVOUR

Aioli

This is one of the great rustic dishes of Provence and is sometimes called 'Le Beurre de Provence'.

Aioli truly produces the magic of the Gulf of St. Tropez.

It is a masterpiece of fish and boiled vegetables served with a strong Aioli sauce (garlic mayonnaise).

It is better served at house parties as the guests are prone to sleep soundly shortly after partaking of this great dish.

A bottle of Sancerre drunk immediately before this dish, greatly helps to prepare the palate!

Serves 6

1 *lb salt cod fish*
6 *potatoes*
6 *sweet potatoes*
6 *courgettes*
1 *lb small carrots*
1 *lb whole French beans*
6 *hard boiled eggs*
6 *ripe tomatoes*
fresh salad

Sauce

4 *large cloves garlic per person*
1 *egg yolk for each 2 people*
olive oil
salt and black pepper
lemon juice

Boil the fish and vegetables separately and the fish should be tender but firm.

Serve the vegetables hot, eggs in their shells and tomatoes raw.

Place fish in centre of large cereal dish.

To make sauce, crush garlic to smooth paste, blend in egg yolks until mixture is smooth, add olive oil and whisk as you would for mayonnaise.

The Aioli will thicken into a firm consistency.

The exact quantity of oil should depend on the number of yolks used.

Season to taste with salt, pepper and lemon juice.

The sauce is served in a large bowl and the guests help themselves.

Aubergine Purée
(Poor Man's Caviar)

My father made this Armenian dish excellently.

3 *aubergines (egg plants)*
4 *tablespoons olive oil*
3 *tablespoons chopped parsley*
2 *cloves garlic, crushed*
juice of 1 *lemon or more*
salt and black pepper to taste

The best way of preparing this purée is to grill the aubergines over charcoal, however, it will probably be more convenient to grill them under a conventional griddle.

Grill until the skins are dark and start to blister and the flesh is soft.

Rub the skins off under a cold tap and remove charred particles.

Place aubergines in a bowl and mash with a fork or pound to a smooth paste in a mortar, (an electric blender will also give good results).

Add the oil, beating all he time.

Then add remaining ingredients and vigorously blend into Purée.

Taste and add more lemon juice, garlic and seasoning as you wish.

Serve with coleslaw or side salad.

AUBERGINES   ILLUSTRATOR: GLYNN BOYD HARTE   67

ZSA ZSA GABOR

Szekely Gulas

Serves 6–8

2 *onions*
1 *tablespoon crisco (cooking oil)*
2 *lb small pieces of pork (off bone)*
2 *lb sauerkraut*
salt
paprika
2 *tsp caraway seed*
1 *lb Hungarian sausage (preferable) or*
Polish sausage
8 *fl oz sour cream*

Sauté minced onions in crisco until light brown.

Add to it the small pieces of pork and simmer for 2 hours.

After this, mix with the sauerkraut, paprika, salt, caraway seed and simmer for about $\frac{1}{2}$ an hour.

Add the Hungarian sausage ($\frac{1}{2}$ inch slices) during the last 10 minutes of simmering.

When ready, add the sour cream and serve.

Zsa Zsa Gábor

ZSA ZSA GABOR   ILLUSTRATOR: NICK TAGGART

MICHAEL MEDWIN

Bstilla
(Moroccan Chicken Pie)

Serves 6–8

2 *poussins or* 1 *large chicken*
2 *tablespoons butter*
1 *large onion, finely chopped or grated*
salt and black pepper
$\frac{1}{2}$ *tsp ground ginger*
$\frac{1}{4}$ *tsp powdered saffron (optional)*
$\frac{1}{2}$ *tsp ground cinnamon*
$\frac{1}{2}$ *tsp mixed spice or ground allspice*
3 *tablespoons finely-chopped parsley*
7–8 *eggs*
6 *oz butter, melted*
16 *sheets fila (Greek pastry available ready-made in Greek grocery shops)*
  1 *tablespoon sugar*
  $\frac{1}{4}$ *tsp ground cinnamon*
  $\frac{1}{4}$ *lb almonds, chopped and sautéed in butter*
  1 *egg yolk, beaten, to glaze*
  little cinnamon and sugar, to garnish

Wash the poussins or chicken.

Quarter them, and simmer in a very little water with butter, onion, seasonings and parsley for about 2 hours, or until the flesh is so tender that it falls off the bones.

Add a little more water as required.

The giblets and liver may be simmered with the birds.

When cooked, drain off the stock and reserve.

Skin and bone the chicken, and cut the meat into smallish pieces.

Take about $\frac{1}{4}$ pint stock and beat it well with the eggs.

Season to taste with salt and pepper, pour into a small pan and stir over a low heat until the mixture is creamy and nearly set.

The eggs and chicken make up the filling of the pie.

Brush a large round (or square) pie tin or oven dish about 13 inches in diameter and $1\frac{1}{2}$–2 inches deep with melted butter.

Fit a sheet of fila in the dish so that the ends fold well up and overlap the edges.

If this is not possible, use overlapping sheets of fila.

Lay 6 sheets of fila on top of each other, brushing melted butter evenly between each layer.

Sprinkle the top layers with sugar, cinnamon and sautéed almonds.

Spread more than half of the egg mixture over this, and sprinkle with a little of the remaining chicken stock.

Cover with another 4 sheets of fila, each one brushed with melted butter.

Lay the pieces of boned chicken neatly on the top and cover with the rest of the egg mixture.

Sprinkle with a little more chicken stock.

Cover with the remaining fila sheets, brushing each layer with melted butter.

Tuck the top fila sheets between the overlapping bottom sheets and the sides of the dish.

Paint the top with beaten egg yolk and bake in a slow to moderate oven (350°F–375°F, gas 3–4) for the first 40 minutes.

Then raise the temperature to 425°F, gas 6 and bake for a further 15 minutes, or until the pastry is crisp and the top a deep golden brown colour.

Serve sprinkled with sugar mixed with cinnamon, and cut, if you like, in a criss-cross pattern of lozenges.

It's delicious.

KATIE BOYLE

Roast Turkey

10–14 lb turkey
thyme and lemon stuffing
lard to baste

Stuff the bird in the neck end (leave the other end empty, making your chestnut stuffing separately) with thyme and lemon stuffing; brush or pour the melted lard over the bird, then place in the oven pre-heated to 425 °F, gas 7.

Baste often, cooking the bird until, when the baking dish is tilted, the juices inside run out clear like water.

This is the most reliable gauge for the cooking time, however large the bird.

I found a 16 lb bird took just under 2 hours before the juices ran clear.

The bird is then cooked—time, approximately 1½ hours.

Any longer cooking will only tend to dry out the turkey and make it slightly stringy.

This method produces marvellous cold turkey.

Brandy & Rum Butter

BRANDY BUTTER
10 oz caster sugar
8 oz butter
brandy

RUM BUTTER

10 oz soft brown sugar
8 oz butter
rum

Melt all the butter in the pan over a low heat.

Do not let it simmer.

When it is just melted, tip in the sugar, remove from the heat, stir well.

Heat a tablespoon, fill with either rum or brandy, pour into the butter and sugar mixture.

Stir until the mixture begins to firm, pour into a container, and allow to set.

This will keep in a cool place for long periods: use as required.

In some areas grated nutmeg is added to the rum butter; this, of course, is optional.

Although this may sound quite impossible, I have *proved* it over the past six years to be the most effective way of cooking turkey.

It was given to me originally by Toni Stopanni, who's responsible for quite a few royal wedding cakes, etc.

The first time I cooked turkey in this way, my husband surreptitiously bought an alternative meal in case things went wrong—he didn't think our guests would be mad about raw turkey!

Katie Boyle

KATIE BOYLE/COLD TURKEY   ILLUSTRATOR: JOHN KOSH

GASP! STIRLING MOSS !!

QUICK, VEAL STROGANOFF AND
MARINATED KIPPERS !!

BAKED BEANS ON TOAST PLEASE !

STIRLING MOSS   ILLUSTRATOR: GRAHAM THOMPSON

STIRLING MOSS

Veal Stroganoff

Serves 4

1 lb boneless veal cutlet
1 teaspoon kitchen bouquet
1 teaspoon salt
1 teaspoon dry mustard
good dash pepper
pinch of marjoram
3 tablespoons fat
1 sliced onion
¼ lb cooked mushrooms
1 tablespoon cornflour
2 tablespoons cold water
½ cup sour cream
2 tablespoons tomato ketchup

Pound the veal until ¼ inch thick, cut into 1 inch strips and place in a bowl.

Sprinkle with bouquet seasoning, dry mustard, and marjoram, tossing lightly with a fork to coat evenly.

Melt the fat in a frying pan over moderate heat, add meat and brown lightly on both sides.

Add the onion and cook for about 5 minutes stirring frequently.

Mix the cornflour and cold water, and pour on the meat.

Now add the cooked mushrooms, sour cream, and ketchup, and warm through for about 10 minutes before serving.

Marinated Kippers

Serves 2

1 small onion, finely cut in rings
1 heaped teaspoon brown sugar
2 pairs kippers, boned and skinned
wine vinegar

Put a thin layer of onion rings in the bottom of a dish and sprinkle with a little sugar.

Then put in a layer of kippers and continue in this way until the dish is full: sprinkle with wine vinegar.

Leave to stand, covered tightly, for 2–4 hours.

Serve with toast or dry biscuits.

To be followed by Super Amplex if the onions are eaten!

RONNIE CORBETT

Bitoxes & Cream Sauce

Makes 6 bitoxes

1 *large onion, chopped*
$2\frac{1}{2}$ *oz butter*
2 *dessertspoons oil*
1 *raw egg*
$1\frac{1}{4}$ *lb best braising steak, minced*
salt and pepper to taste
$\frac{1}{4}$ *teaspoon thyme*

SAUCE
$\frac{1}{2}$ *beef stock cube*
1 *cup boiling water*
$\frac{1}{2}$ *pint double cream*

To make bitoxes, fry onion in $1\frac{1}{2}$ oz butter and 1 dessertspoon oil.

Simmer until soft but not brown.

Mix egg with minced meat and add salt, pepper, and thyme.

Mix in onion when soft.

Divide mixture into six and roll together as for meatballs.

Place in the fridge to harden.

Fry in the remaining butter and oil for about 8 minutes turning twice.

When cooked, keep warm in oven.

To make sauce, throw out the fat from the pan and add stock cube in boiling water.

Stir over heat until the cube is completely dissolved and then add cream.

Boil for a few minutes to reduce.

Pour over the bitoxes and serve.

My wife, Anne, is such a good cook, that when she joined Womens Lib, she didn't burn her bra, she sautéed it with onions and white wine!

RONNIE CORBETT   ILLUSTRATOR: JOSEPH WRIGHT

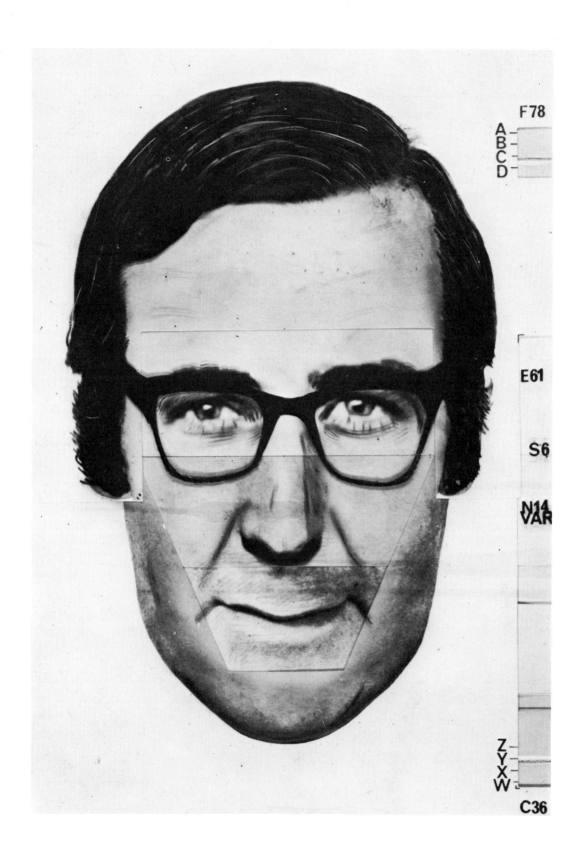

SHAW TAYLOR   PHOTO-FIT: DET. SGT. J. A. TALBOT, NEW SCOTLAND YARD

SHAW TAYLOR

Braised Oxtails

Serves 6–8

1 *oxtail*
1 *lb onions*
1 *lb carrots*
2 *sticks celery*
fat for frying
salt and pepper
4 *oz flour*
4 *oz tomato purée*
4 *pints beef stock*
bouquet garni
½ *lb fatty bacon*
½ *lb mushrooms*

Trim the heavy fat from thick end of tail, and cut in sections through the joints.

These can be found by locating the slight lump at about 2 inch intervals along the tail.

Peel and chop the vegetables into 1 inch dice, and fry the seasoned oxtail in a heavy pan with little fat until brown.

Add the vegetables, and brown lightly.

Add flour and cook for a few minutes but do not allow to burn.

Add the tomato purée, stock, bouquet garni, chopped bacon, and mushrooms.

Check seasoning.

Cover with a tightly fitting lid, and cook gently in the oven (325 °F, gas 3) for 3–4 hours, or until the meat is tender and leaves the bone easily.

Check that the stock does not evaporate too much, and skim off any fat.

Remove bouquet garni before serving.

Cooking time will depend on the tails but usually 3–4 hours is sufficient.

The problem at our dinner parties is that we talk too much, and so do all our friends.

The gay and witty comment mixes with the deep and serious to make the 'party' part of the dinner party great.

It's the dinner part that suffers.

From my wife's point of view, there is nothing more frustrating than having to keep an eye on what's happening in the kitchen when she knows there are so many things she would like to be saying in the sitting room.

Our answer and our saviour is Braised Oxtails.

The slave is released from the kitchen because all can be prepared before the guests arrive.

It's the perfect answer—except that, 'he who says least, eats most!'

JOHNNY MATHIS

Wild Duck

Serves 4–6

2 or 3 wild ducks
salt and pepper
½ cup* onion, chopped
1 green pepper, sliced
2 or 3 celery stalks, cut
3 cups* water

Clean the ducks.
Rub with salt and pepper.
Place in baking pan, breast side up.
Add the onion, pepper slices, celery, and water to the pan.
Cover, and bake at 325 °F, gas 3 for 2 hours, or until the ducks are tender.
Baste occasionally.
Serve on a bed of wild rice.

The secret of this recipe is choosing ducks fed only on grain or rice.
They are not as fishy tasting!
*1 cup = 8 fl oz

LEG OF LAMB   DESIGNER: MARCELLO MINALE

VICTOR SPINETTI

Agnello di Turco

leg of lamb (New Zealand will do)
2 teaspoons olive oil
½ teaspoon red pepper
½ teaspoon black pepper
1 clove garlic
crushed thyme

Skin the leg.

Cover skinned leg with the oil (very sexy to do), and the pepper.

Rub into the lamb.

Cut up the garlic, and insert pieces into the leg where you fancy.

Smother the rubbed, oiled and garlic stuffed leg (see what I mean about sexy) in thyme.

Cover the pan in foil, and put in the oven at 350 °F, gas 4, for 1 hour.

Then remove foil, and cook for another hour.

This will make any old leg into a dainty, tasty dish.

Perhaps we should call it Leg of Lamb Mistinguette (spelling wrong, but you know what I mean).

Victor Spinetti

TONY RICHARDSON

Loup au Nid du Duc

Serves 8–10

4–6 *lb loup (sea bass or other comparable fish)*
salt and pepper
herbs (fennel, thyme, celery leaves)
2 *lemons, sliced in rounds*
4 *oz butter*
olive oil
2 *onions, minced*
4 *celery stalks, minced*
3 *cups mayonnaise*
5 *tablespoons capers*
1 *large cucumber, peeled and thinly sliced*
1 *slice tomato*
1 *slice hardboiled egg*
bits of black olive
bits of pimiento

Place the loup in a baking dish, season the cavity, and stuff it with a few sprigs of herbs.

From head to tail, slice through to the backbone at 2 inch intervals and insert lemon rounds and butter.

Douse with some olive oil and bake in a moderate oven (350 °F, gas 4) for about 30 minutes, until flaky but still moist.

Baste occasionally with liquids from the pan.

(The fish is also delicious when eaten hot.)

When the fish cools, separate all the meat from the skin and bones.

Chill the meat overnight.

The next day break it into bite-size pieces.

Add minced onions and celery stalks.

Stir in $1\frac{1}{2}$ cups mayonnaise, the capers, and salt and pepper to taste.

Toss lightly, and mould it into a fish shape on a long dish.

Starting at the tail end, arrange the cucumber slices in overlapping rows until $\frac{2}{3}$ up the body, to look like scales.

Cover the rest with mayonnaise, create a huge fish eye using 1 tomato slice topped with 1 smaller slice of hardboiled egg and a bit of black olive.

Use bits of pimiento to make the lips.

Garnish the platter as you wish, and serve the totally edible fish with the rest of the mayonnaise.

This cold fish recipe is fun to make, spectacular to look at, delicious to eat and can be made well in advance.

SEA BASS   DESIGNER: SAUL BASS

JILL BENNETT   ILLUSTRATOR: WILLIAM RANKIN

JILL BENNETT

Cassoulet

Serves 6

¾ *lb haricot beans*
few bacon bones
2 *lb boiling bacon*
½ *garlic sausage, diced*
6 *strong onions, chopped and lightly sautéed*
¾ *lb black mushrooms*
1 *medium-sized part-roasted chicken, diced*
6 *lamb cutlets*
2 *bay leaves*
salt and pepper

Soak the beans overnight, then drain.

Put the bacon bones and bacon in a *large* saucepan, and cover with water.

Bring to the boil, skim, and then simmer for 1 hour, or until the stock has a good strong flavour.

Grease a large casserole, and line it with the beans.

Add the garlic sausage, onions, mushrooms, chicken, cutlets, boiled bacon carved into six portions, stock, bay leaves and seasoning (but go easy on the salt initially).

Then cook in a slow oven (250 °F, gas ½) for as long as possible!

Quite a lot of effort is involved but it ought to be worth it.

Very nourishing but not for the low calorie and lettuce brigade!

Jill Bennett

DONALD PLEASENCE

Shrimp Curry

Serves 4

To make the curry sauce—put 1 teaspoon ground dhaniya, 2 teaspoons ground tumeric, and ½ teaspoon chili powder in a saucepan.

Add 1 tablespoon butter and ½ teaspoon ginger, salt, pepper, and ground garlic.

When the butter has melted, add ½ pint milk and 2 tablespoons cream, and stir until yellow.

Take 1 lb peeled shrimps, cook them in butter in the oven (325 °F, gas 3) for 10 minutes, and add to the curry sauce.

Cook for another 15 minutes in the oven.

Just before serving spread the curry with shredded coconut under the grill until lightly brown.

Serve with a bowl of rice.

When we were in India a beautiful Indian lady taught my wife to make curry properly.

This is one of her recipes.

DONALD PLEASANCE   ILLUSTRATOR: JULIAN ALLEN

A CHILLIED TASTE BUD   ILLUSTRATOR: KENNY EVERETT

KENNY EVERETT

Creamed Chillied Kidneys with Spaghetti

Serves 4–6

½ oz butter
1 clove garlic
1 lb lamb's kidney
1 glass dry sherry
1 tsp mustard
1 tsp chilli powder
1 handful grated parsley
coarse salt
4 oz heavy cream
1 lb spaghetti

Heat butter with chopped garlic.

Add cleaned and chopped kidneys and juice, cook for a few minutes, add sherry and let reduce.

Add mustard, chilli powder and parsley.

Season to taste.

Add cream and let it warm through —don't boil, serve on spaghetti and sprinkle with Parmesan cheese.

There are only two things you can do with kidneys. Donate them or cream them.

My wife usually serves this fabulous recipe to visiting T.V. executives.

Soon after this, contracts pour in like confetti.

Lee's Creamed Chillied Kidneys have often saved our marriage, as the thought of never having it again has struck horror into the very heart of my taste buds.

You *must* try this recipe.

It'll make a new man of you . . . even if you're a woman.

JOE JANNI

Pasta North-Centre

Serves 4

1 *lb short pasta*
1 *onion*
oil and butter for frying
8 *tomatoes*
1 *oz dried mushrooms (1 small packet per person)*
basil
thyme
oregano
rosemary
savory
sage
Fontina cheese
unsalted butter

First make the usual tomato sauce by chopping the onion very, very fine, frying it in oil and butter mixed, and then adding the peeled and de-pipped tomatoes.

In a separate pan, cook the dried mushrooms in butter (make sure they have been soaked for at least 2 hours, and also cut small), and when they begin to change colour, add all the herbs.

Allow both sauces to cook gently for around 45 minutes.

While the pasta is being cooked, heat a bowl until it is very hot.

When the pasta is almost ready put small pieces of a Piemontese cheese called Fontina into the hot bowl.

Then add the drained pasta (which will melt the cheese), and put in a lot of unsalted butter.

Pour both sauces over all this and mix together.

If you are on a slimming diet, eat a dozen grapefruit without sugar before eating 'My Pasta'!

This is a mixture of recipes from Piemonte and from Tuscany.

The best pasta to use is a short-type, ideally Gnocchi Sardi which cannot be found in England though you can get it in most Italian cities.

If you cannot get it, use Penne Rigate.

92

JOE JANNI   ILLUSTRATOR: ARNOLD SCHWARTZMAN

WHITELAW'S GOULASH   DESIGNER: ALAN FLETCHER

BILLIE WHITELAW

Whitelaw's Goulash

Serves 6–8

Take 4 lb braising steak and cut it into cubes the size of a thumb.

Put a tiny cube of lard into a large saucepan or casserole and add 2 lb chopped onions (not less!).

Brown the meat and onions over a fairly strong heat, and then turn down as low as possible.

Add 4 oz chopped bacon, as much paprika as you can enjoy, ½ eggcup caraway seed, 1 whole tube tomato purée, salt and a little cayenne pepper.

Let this simmer for about 3 hours, turn off your stove, and forget it.

Next day: start again, letting the goulash simmer over a very low flame until the meat is tender and the onions and other goodies have turned into a rich, red-brown gravy.

The trick is not to overcook the meat.

If there is time, don't eat it even on the second day, but let it cool overnight, and warm it up on the third day.

For some mysterious reason, a goulash tastes better if it has been left to stand, but never let it bubble or boil.

It tastes great with rice, into which you mix some peas and fine slices of red pepper.

As a side dish, I suggest very thinly sliced cucumber salad.

When it succeeds, it's so tasty that guests usually ask for second helpings.

This is a recipe my husband, Robert Muller, taught me.

It's something we both like to eat, and is useful to cook when you're expecting people, but don't know how many.

Billie

LAURENCE HARVEY

Chicken Pie

Serves 4

1 *chicken*
1½ *pints water*
½ *lb bacon*
salt and pepper
1 *onion, sliced*
½ *lb mushrooms, sliced*
parsley
3 *leaves gelatine*
2 *hardboiled eggs*
flaky pastry

Bone and cut the chicken into convenient sized pieces.

Make a good strong stock with the carcass and water, then strain off and allow to cool before making the pie.

Line the pie dish with the slices of bacon.

Season the pieces of chicken well.

Mix the onion, mushrooms and parsley together and add a little chicken stock with 1 gelatine leaf to help set.

Put the ingredients in the pie dish in layers of chicken, onion and mushroom mix, hardboiled egg etc.

Then fill the dish with stock, reserving a little for the aspic.

Cover with pastry and decorate.

Bake in a hot oven (425 °F, gas 7) for approximately 35 minutes, with a piece of grease-proof paper wrapped around the pie.

Then decrease the heat of the oven, and continue cooking for about 1 hour.

Leave to stand but while warm, coat the pastry with some chicken aspic made with the rest of the chicken stock boiled with remaining leaves of gelatine, and allowed to cool slightly.

Yummy for the tummy.

Laurence Harvey

STUFFED VINE LEAVES   ARTIST: HARRIET FREEDMAN

CAT STEVENS

Dolmades (Stuffed Vine Leaves)

*vine leaves (obtainable from Greek food
shops in Soho)*
$\frac{1}{2}$ *lb mince, cooked*
$\frac{1}{4}$ *cup rice, cooked*
1 onion, chopped
*1 teaspoon each freshly chopped parsley
and mint*
1 beaten egg
seasoning to taste

SAUCE

2 lemons
1 small tin tomatoes
1 tablespoon tomato purée
$\frac{1}{4}$ *pint good stock*
seasoning to taste

Blanch the vine leaves in boiling
salted water, and set aside to drain.

Bind the remaining ingredients together, and place a small portion on
each of the vine leaves.

Roll each leaf around the mixture,
and secure the parcels with a cocktail
stick.

Place the bundles in a buttered oven-
proof dish.

Squeeze juice of 1 lemon over the
dolmades.

Chop the tomatoes, and mix these
with purée, stock and seasoning.

Pour the sauce over the dolmades,
and cover with a small plate or saucer
to prevent them moving during
cooking.

Place in a moderate oven (350 °F,
gas 4) for about 30 minutes.

Serve with generous wedges of
lemon.

They can be served either hot or cold
as desired.

N.B. If all this sounds a bit of a drag,
dolmades are canned to perfection, and
can be obtained from that well-known
food hall in Knightsbridge!

OMAR SHARIF

Morgan Barid
(Cold Mullet)

This is a well-known Egyptian recipe.

fresh mullet
coarse kitchen salt
olive oil
black pepper
1 clove garlic
some fresh ripe tomatoes
1 small onion
parsley
small glass white wine or juice of 2/3 lemons
1 slice orange or lemon

Wash the mullet carefully.
Rub inside and out with coarse salt.
Peel the tomatoes and slice thickly.
Chop onion very finely and chop the garlic coarsely.
Brown the mullet in olive oil, season to taste with black pepper and salt.
Place the tomatoes in a fireproof dish and the browned fish on top.
Stuff the fish with onions, garlic and chopped parsley.
Pour on the wine or lemon juice.
Cover and cook in a moderate oven (350°F, gas 4) until the flesh of the fish will part at the touch of a fork.
Serve with chopped parsley on top and surround with sliced orange or lemon.
Offer aubergine pickle as a side dish.
Serve with yoghurt salad.

HARRY ANDREWS

Poulet à L'Estragon

Serves 4–6

fresh tarragon
2 oz butter
salt and pepper
3 lb roasting chicken
1 tsp flour
¼ pt double cream

This is essentially a summer dish, as it can only be made with fresh tarragon.

Mix a tablespoon of chopped tarragon leaves with 2 ounces of softened butter, season with salt and pepper, and stuff the chicken with this mixture.

Cook the chicken in butter in a thick covered casserole until tender.

The bird should be laid on its side, and turned over half way through the cooking and basted.

When tender, remove to a serving dish and stir into the juices in the pan a walnut of butter worked with the flour.

When this has amalgamated, add the cream and two tablespoons of chopped tarragon.

Bring to the boil, and when it has thickened, pour over the chicken and serve.

Harry Andrews.

HARRY ANDREWS   ILLUSTRATOR: GIANNETTO COPPOLA

SALADE COMPOSE   ILLUSTRATOR: TERRY GRIFFITHS

RUSSELL HARTY

Salade Composé

This dish takes approximately 4 minutes to prepare once the ingredients are gathered together upon the melamine working surface.

Before that, it will take approximately a weekend, or a week, or a month, depending upon your ability to get, as it were, things together.

Gather a lettuce or some of that blood-red green leaf which the French call lettuce.

Wash it.

Open a tin of sweetcorn.

Chop up a green pepper.

Slice thinly the pumpkin-sized tomatoes the French call '*tomates*'.

Swill all this around in a deep bowl with lumps of garlic and 2 teaspoonsful of walnut oil from the Périgord.

Finally, open a tin of foie gras, slice that thinly and lay it gently upon the top of the mixed salad.

The reason why it all takes a long time to collect is that you are, quite reasonably, required to go to the source for the materials, and you might as well enjoy yourself doing it.

With travel and overnight expenses added, the mouthsful start working out at something like £87.30 plus V.A.T., so I sincerely hope you enjoy it.

Russell Harty

TOM CONTI

Chicken à la Mama Conti

Serves 4

Take one fresh chicken, rub with olive oil and sprinkle fairly liberally with salt.

Slice three medium-sized onions, turn in oil and lay rings on chicken.

Place in medium oven and cook.

I don't know how long it takes; I am an actor, not a Liberal M.P.

Sometimes it's overdone, sometimes it's underdone.

You might be lucky.

The important bit comes now.

Empty the juices by tilting the chicken towards its rear end.

This is the famous schmaltz—the juices, not the rear end.

When you serve the chicken, dip the pieces in the schmaltz.

Serve with what's left of unburned onions.

Actually, if you baste the chicken regularly through cooking, the onions won't all be burned.

I like this with roast potatoes.

Just sling a few potatoes around about the chicken as it's cooking. Make sure to keep basting them.

The actual work involved in this dish should not take more than five minutes.

If it does, then I suggest you take up membership in Parliament.

Good luck.

Salut!

Tom Conti.

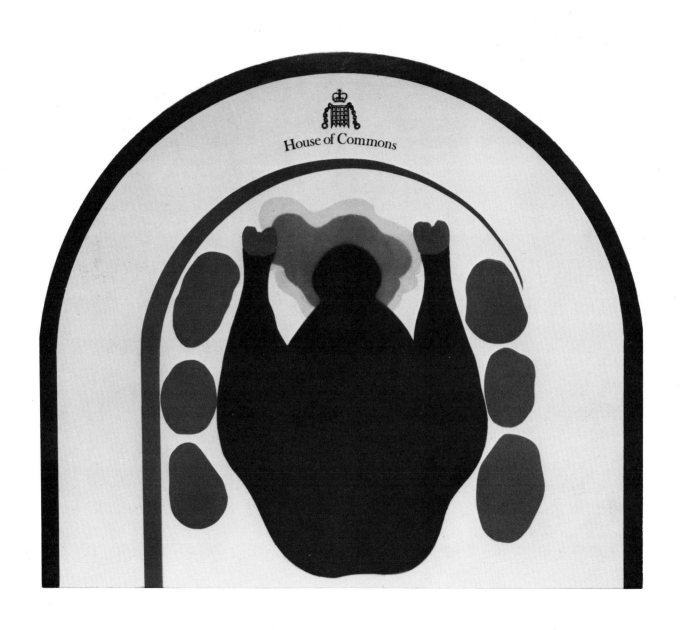

CHICKEN À LA MAMA CONTI   ILLUSTRATOR: COLIN CHEESEMAN

DIMITRI TIOMKIN

Beef Stroganoff

Serves 4–6

$\frac{1}{2}$ lb fresh sliced mushrooms
1 large onion, finely chopped
4 tablespoons butter
2 lb beef
flour
1 tablespoon salt
2 tins consommé
1 cup sour cream

Sauté the mushrooms and onion in 2 tablespoons butter until brown.

Remove from the pan.

Chop the meat, and roll in flour.

Put the remaining butter in a different pan with the meat, and cook until brown.

Then add salt and the consommé.

Cook on a low heat for $1\frac{1}{2}$–2 hours, stirring occasionally, and adding extra water, if necessary.

Stir in the mushrooms and onions, and last of all, the sour cream.

Serve with rice or noodles.

This recipe is workable providing using sufficient amount of good wine ... best!!!

Dimitri Tiomkin

DIMITRI TIOMKIN   PHOTOGRAPHER: STEPHEN COE

ERIC AMBLER/STUFFED GREEN PEPPER   ILLUSTRATOR: BERNARD LODGE

ERIC AMBLER

Stuffed Green Peppers

6 *medium-sized green peppers*
1 *lb minced beef*
1 *small finely chopped onion*
1 *tablespoon shortening*
1 *lb tin tomatoes*
1 *cup cooked rice*
1 *tablespoon Worcester sauce*
2 *tablespoons parsley, finely chopped*
1 *teaspoon salt*
$\frac{1}{8}$ *teaspoon pepper*
1 *cup grated Cheddar cheese*

Cut the tops off the peppers, and remove the seeds and membranes.

Cook for 5 minutes in rapidly boiling salted water.

Brown the meat and onion lightly in shortening.

Add 1 cup of the tomatoes, the rice, Worcester sauce, parsley, and seasoning.

Cook and stir for 2–3 minutes.

Add $\frac{1}{2}$ cup cheese, and mix.

Stand the peppers upright in a baking dish.

Spoon filling into peppers, and pour round the remaining tomatoes.

Sprinkle with the cheese, and bake uncovered at 350 °F, gas 4, for 25 minutes.

Serve.

This is a light supper dish which we like to eat at home.

One of its merits is that the cook has 25 minutes clear in which to have a pre-food drink.

You serve Gravlax either as a starter, thinly sliced on toast, or as a main dish in thick slices, with new potatoes and green salad—and the all important Dilled Mustard Sauce.

There are almost as many different recipes for the Swedish Gravlax as there are Gravlax fans.

This is the recipe my Swedish wife has settled on after many experiments.

Don't be put off by the details, it's worth the bother.

Gravlax

I usually prepare a whole salmon since it can be kept in the fridge or grilled, etc.

But for this recipe I'll use 2 lb salmon to indicate the proportions.

The salmon should be fresh, but you can use Canadian frozen salmon which does nearly as well for much less money.

The Canadian salmon shouldn't be completely de-frosted—only sufficiently to allow you to remove the big bones.

You could rub the almost de-frosted salmon with a few drips of gin, and then brush with cooking oil before preparing it.

Two snags for making Gravlax in England: it is difficult to buy fresh dill (in which case dried dill will have to do), and for the mustard sauce you need sweet mustard, which I have only located at the Norwegian foodplace in Knightsbridge.

The cut should be from the centre of the fish.

Cut in two, length-wise, and have it filleted.

Remove as many bones as possible.

Mix 1 oz sugar, and 1 oz salt with 15 crushed white peppercorns (per 2 lb salmon).

Rub this mixture into the salmon pieces on both sides.

Place the fish on a porcelain or glass dish, flesh sides together, with lots and lots of fresh dill in between.

Arrange the slices so that the thick end of one slice is against the thin end of the other slice.

Place more dill beneath the fish, and dill on top.

Cover the fish with plastic film (it's quite smelly), and put in the fridge for at least 36 hours before it is to be served, turning the packet every time you pass the fridge.

The more it's turned the better it will become.

Remove the salmon from the fridge 2–3 hours before it is to be served—and just before that magic moment it should be cleaned of all the old dill and peppercorns.

Place the salmon slim-side down on a cutting board, and cut it loose from the shin in thin strips or thick slices.

Remove any small bones which may have been left; you will find that they come away quite easily now.

Dilled Mustard Sauce

2 tablespoons chopped dill
1 tablespoon sugar
1 tablespoon sweet mustard
½ tablespoon dark French mustard
1 tablespoon vinegar
4 oz cooking oil

Mix the dill and sugar in a bowl.

Add mustard and vinegar, and mix well.

Beat in oil a little at a time until the sauce has the consistency of thin mayonnaise.

Pour into a sauce dish, and sprinkle with more chopped dill if you wish.

Gravlax should be preceded and accompanied by Aquavit (Scandinavian Schnapps) and washed down with lager, at least in England; Swedes drink dry white wine with it.

Hoppas det smakar bra!!

Christina Burton

Looking forward to eating the rest of the book . . .

Humphrey Burton

GRAVLAX   PHOTOGRAPHER: ALAN BOYD

TURKEY DRESSING   DESIGN TEAM: PATRICIA OLESKO, NEIL SELKIRK,
RICHARD WEIGAND

DAVID SUSSKIND

Dressing for 20 lb Turkey
(1 cup for each lb of turkey)

My wife, Joyce, is a superb cook but my very favourite among her assorted masterpieces is this recipe for turkey dressing.

I have seen with my own eyes grown people rendered immobile with pleasure and gluttony.

It's one hell of a recipe and I recommend it without reservation.

Determine how much rice is required for the amount of dressing needed for the turkey (2 packets long grain and wild rice makes about 6 cups* of rice).

This is doubled when other ingredients are added, but 12 cups* is not too much of this dressing.

STEP ONE

8 *oz packet chicken livers*
giblets from turkey or chicken (omitting gizzard)
5 *cups* chicken stock*
$\frac{1}{2}$ *teaspoon salt*
2 *packets long grain and wild rice (add extra wild rice, if possible)*

Chop the livers and giblets.

Bring the stock to boiling point, adding salt.

Drop the livers and giblets into the water, and simmer for about 10 minutes.

Remove livers and giblets from stock, and set aside.

Stir in the rice and cook according to packet directions.

STEP TWO

$\frac{1}{4}$ *cup* butter or margarine*
$\frac{1}{4}$ *cup* chopped shallots*
1 *cup* chopped onions*
$\frac{1}{2}$ *cup* chopped green pepper*
$\frac{1}{2}$ *cup* chopped celery*
$\frac{1}{2}$ *cup* chopped mushrooms*
salt and freshly ground black pepper
$\frac{1}{2}$ *teaspoon thyme*
$\frac{1}{2}$ *teaspoon sage*
$\frac{1}{4}$ *teaspoon rosemary*
1 *cup* chopped water chestnuts*
1 *cup* pignole nuts*
$\frac{1}{2}$ *cup* finely chopped walnuts*

While the rice is cooking, melt butter or margarine in a large skillet.

Add shallots, onions, green pepper, celery, and mushrooms.

Sauté gently until onions and celery are transparent.

Season to taste, then add the rest of the ingredients and mix well.

STEP THREE

Add the hot drained rice, the chicken livers, and $\frac{1}{2}$ cup* tomato purée.

Season to taste—this is very important.

* 1 *cup* = 8 *fl oz*

113

JOAN COLLINS

Pommes Paysanne or Peasant Potatoes (not for peasants)

Caviar being at a premium these days, this is a luxurious dish (my favourite) in which to indulge oneself, or a select few of one's nearest and dearest.

Bake several medium-sized baking potatoes in tin foil in the oven (350 °F, gas 4) for about 1 hour having scrubbed them thoroughly with a stiff brush to remove all soil.

When cooled, remove foil, split potatoes and mash in 1 ounce of un-salted butter.

Then add as much fresh Beluga Caviar as your palate desires, and top with sour cream (preferably the American kind).

With this serve ice cold Russian Vodka in liqueur glasses.

Better have plenty of caviar on hand as this dish goes like hot cakes.

And do it soon before the caviar supplies run out!

Red Bean Salad

This recipe is for people who give parties but don't like to cook.

Take 2 cans of dark red pinto beans (made in Mexico if possible).

Drain well and throw into a bowl.

Fry 4 large red onions in butter until golden brown.

When cold, add to the beans.

Then add 3 cartons of sour cream.

Mix thoroughly, season to taste with salt and pepper and refrigerate until your guests arrive.

This goes well with all kinds of cold cuts and a plain green salad, and no one will believe it is so easy to make.

Bon Appetit!

JOAN COLLINS ILLUSTRATOR: SUE COE

QUINN MARTIN   ILLUSTRATOR: MARTIN LAMBIE-NAIRN

QUINN MARTIN

Chicken Fiesta Casserole

Serves 10–12

6 *whole chicken breasts (big)*
1 *tsp salt*
1 *dozen corn tortillas (flat package)*
2 *Spanish onions, chopped fine*
1 *7½ oz jar green chili salsa*
1 *4 oz can Ortega whole green chiles (seeded)*
1 *10¾ oz can cream of mushroom soup*
1 *10¾ oz can cream of chicken soup*
1 *pt sour cream*
salt and pepper
½–1 lb Cheddar cheese, grated

Butter a 3 quart casserole or 9½ inch by 13 inch Pyrex dish.

In a large saucepan cover chicken breasts with salted water and simmer until fork tender.

Remove from water and cool.

Remove bones and cut into bite-size pieces.

Pre-heat oven to 325 °F, gas 3.

Tear tortillas into small pieces.

Combine onions, chili salsa, chopped green chiles, mushroom soup, chicken soup, sour cream and season according to taste.

To assemble, layer half of torn tortillas on the bottom of the casserole.

Layer half of chicken and half of sauce.

Sprinkle half of cheese on top of this.

Repeat layers again, ending with cheese.

Cover and refrigerate for 24 hours.

Before baking, bring casserole to room temperature.

Remove cover and bake for 1½ hours.

GEORGIA BROWN

Chili Con Carne

Serves 8–10

2 *tablespoons butter*
2 *tablespoons olive oil*
2 *lb minced beef*
1 *lb minced pork (pork must be good)*
2 *bottles chili seasoning (each 1⅝ oz)*
1 *clove garlic, crushed (adjust to taste)*
3 *large spanish onions*
4 *tins chili beans (each 8 oz)*
little chili paste to taste
1 *large can tomatoes (about 20 oz)*
4 *tablespoons wine vinegar*
Tabasco to taste

Most people fry the onions first but I don't because they make a liquid, then the meat makes soup which de-flavours.

So the thing to do is heat the butter and oil together in a very large pan.

Put in the beef and pork together.

You might feel that too much fat is absorbed and want to add more.

Don't because the pork will sweat and make more fat.

As the meat browns (changing from pink to a darker shade) add chili seasoning and mix quickly until all the meat is coloured by the powder.

By the way, keep the heat fairly high.
Add garlic.
Everything to be done fast.
Mix.
Cut 1 onion small, and mix through the meat.
Add the chili beans and a little chili paste.
Turn down the heat.
Mix again.
Add the can of tomatoes and mix.
Add 3 tablespoons wine vinegar, and if you like chili really hot, add tabasco to taste.
Mix well and cook for 5 minutes—nice and bubbly.

Add 1 more onion chopped fairly coarsely.
Cover $\frac{9}{10}$ of the area, and reduce the heat.
Simmer for 1 hour stirring every 10 minutes unless you possess a really tough iron-bottomed pan.

The heat must be evenly distributed, and you mustn't allow any of the ingredients to stick.

When everybody is ready and the chili tastes right, you can then chop the last onion and leave it raw for serving with the remaining wine vinegar or you can mix it through according to how well you know your audience.

Alongside this dish I take one raw, thickly sliced cucumber.
Mix a small jar of sour cream and yoghurt together.
Pepper the cucumber slightly with anything (eg saffron or dill).
Keep in the refrigerator unmixed until ready to serve.
I also serve with hot French bread and plain white rice to help take away the heat for those guests unused to spicy food.
In summer, serve with an accompaniment of seasonal fruits.

Either drink beer or Spanish red wine—excellent!

This is a *quick* way of making Chili Con Carne without loss of taste given to me by my grandmother.

GEORGIA BROWN   ILLUSTRATOR: DONNA MUIR

TIMPANA   ILLUSTRATOR: EVIE BRICUSSE

EVIE AND LESLIE BRICUSSE

Timpana

Timpana—like Evie—is a well-known old Maltese dish.

Serves 8

1 *aubergine*
$\frac{1}{4}$ *lb butter.*
2 *onions, chopped*
$1\frac{1}{2}$ *lb pork and beef minced meat (half of each)*
1 *lb chicken livers*
4 *or* 5 *mushrooms*
2 *or* 3 *cloves of garlic (according to taste)*
mixed herbs
black ground pepper
salt
8 *oz tomato purée*
meat stock or cubes
5 *raw eggs*
$\frac{1}{2}$ *pt milk*
$1\frac{1}{2}$ *lb long thick round macaroni, snapped in half*
$1\frac{1}{2}$ *lb puff or short pastry*
$\frac{1}{2}$ *lb ricotta or cottage cheese*
4 *hard-boiled eggs*
$\frac{1}{4}$ *lb Parmesan cheese, grated*

Peel the aubergine and cut into small pieces.

Using a saucepan, fry in butter with chopped onions.

Add the minced meats, chicken livers, mushrooms, garlic, herbs, salt and pepper.

Sauté the mixture.

Thin the tomato purée with a little stock.

Add to the contents of the saucepan and simmer.

Beat the eggs and milk together and put to one side.

Boil the macaroni in plenty of salted water until barely tender and do not overcook.

Rinse and drain.

Grease a deep baking dish and line the bottom and sides with thin pastry.

Mix the contents of the saucepan into the macaroni.

Fold in ricotta or cottage cheese and put the whole mixture in the pastry-lined baking dish.

Slice the hard-boiled eggs and place on top.

Add the egg-and-milk mixture and sprinkle with Parmesan cheese, saving some to garnish, spreading all over and allowing to seep through. Cover with pastry.

Cook in a moderate oven for $1-1\frac{1}{2}$ hours.

Let it stand for 20 minutes before serving.

Garnish with grated Parmesan cheese.

Cut and serve in square portions in similar style to lasagne, together with any form of salad to suit.

It is important to prepare and cook the dish en croute, whether or not you eat the pastry.

SAMMY DAVIS JNR.

Sammy's Leg of Pork

There are three things I love—my home, the stage and the White Elephant.

Whenever I come to England I know this dish is there waiting for me.

Serves 10–12

½ leg of pork (about 8 lb)
salt

Score the pork and salt well, rubbing it into the meat as well.

Place in a moderate oven (350 °F, gas 3) for about 3 hours.

Serve with crackling which will be crispy if cooked gently, together with apple sauce and stuffing. There is no need to use any fat.

Apple Sauce

2 lb cooking apples (Bramley's if possible)
4 oz granulated sugar

Peel and core the apples. Place in a saucepan with sugar and enough water to cover.

Cook thoroughly and pass through a sieve before serving.

Stuffing

1 large onion
1 teaspoon rubbed sage
4 oz butter
8 oz breadcrumbs
salt and pepper

Chop onion finely and cook gently without colour in butter until tender.

Add the remainder of the ingredients.

Mix well and serve.

LEG OF PORK/SAMMY DAVIS JNR.   ILLUSTRATOR: DAVID POCKNELL

QUEEN VICTORIA/BACON ROLL PUDDING   ILLUSTRATOR: PETER BROOKES

LORD MILES

Bacon Roll Pudding

One of my grandmothers was born in Kirkcudbright in a village called Glen Lochar near Castle Douglas, and worked as a housemaid in Balmoral back in the 1850's. During her tenure there she formed a close friendship with Charlie Francatelli who was chief cook to Queen Victoria, and she copied down many recipes of his which were passed to my mother and so on to Josephine and myself. One in particular was a favourite with Her Majesty, viz. Bacon Roll Pudding and this recipe is exactly as it has been passed down to our own kitchen, where we also, and our children and grandchildren greatly enjoy it.

Serves 4

1 *lb finest bacon*
6 *apples (sliced)*
1 *onion (sliced)*
2 *lb flour*
herbs

Boil the bacon for half an hour, and then cut it into thin slices.

Make flour into a stiff dough by adding water, roll it out thin, then lay the slices of apple and the slices of onion; sprinkle with herbs.

Roll up the paste so as to secure the bacon etc. in it, and place the bolster pudding in a cloth, tied at each end, and let it boil for 2 hours in a 2-gallon pot, with plenty of water.

Bunn

Now Lord Miles of Blackfriars of course!

WILLIS HALL

Lancashire Hot-Pot

Serves 4

2 lb best neck end
sprinkling of pearl barley
1 lb carrots
1 large onion, sliced
2 lb potatoes
stock
dripping

Place the cutlets in the bottom of a casserole.

Add the pearl barley, carrots and sliced onion.

Slice the potatoes, and arrange them neatly on top of the vegetables.

Add a slightly thickened stock, leaving the top layer of the potatoes exposed.

Place small pieces of dripping on the top layer of sliced potatoes.

Cover the casserole, and cook slowly in the oven (275 °F, gas 1) for 2 hours.

Remove the cover and place the casserole in the hottest part of the oven, raising the heat to 350 °F, gas 4, and cook for another 20 minutes, or until the top layer of potatoes is brown and crisp.

As a true Yorkshireman, I hold firmly to the belief that the only good things to come out of Lancashire are hot-pot and very fast trains.

The recipe for the hot-pot is printed above; the times of the fast trains out of Lancashire can be found by referring to local timetables!

WILLIS HALL   PHOTOGRAPHER: PETER HOWE

MALCOLM ARNOLD

Chicken with Rosemary

Serves 4

1 *small chicken, jointed*
salt and freshly ground pepper
oil for frying
4 *slices green bacon, diced*
2 *cloves garlic, pressed*
$\frac{1}{4}$ *pint dry white wine*
$\frac{1}{4}$ *pint chicken stock*
1 *dessertspoon fresh rosemary, finely chopped*

Season the chicken joints, and fry in oil in an oven-proof casserole until crisp, together with bacon and garlic.

Pour over the wine and stock, sprinkle with rosemary and allow to bubble for a moment or two.

Season again if required.

Cover and cook for 1 hour in a moderate oven (350 °F, gas 4), until tender.

Do not drink all the Soave and Valpollicella while cooking; save some to drink with it!

GLYNIS JOHNS

Chicken Paprika

Serves 4

4 *chicken joints*
seasoned flour
vegetable oil
1 *onion, sliced*
$\frac{1}{4}$ *lb mushrooms, sliced*
$\frac{1}{2}$ *lb carrots, sliced $\frac{1}{3}$ inch thick*
1 *lb potatoes, sliced*
paprika
salt and pepper
little single cream
1 *pint milk*

Skin and wash the chicken joints, dry, and sprinkle with seasoned flour.

Heat the oil in a frying pan, add the onion and chicken joints.

Simmer, turning the joints, until the onions are light gold.

Take a casserole and place in it a layer of chicken joints and onion, followed by a layer of mushrooms and carrots, then a layer of sliced potatoes.

(These vegetables can be varied according to personal taste.)

Sprinkle with paprika, salt and pepper to taste.

Make a slightly thickened white sauce by adding a little cream to the milk, and pour over the contents.

Put a lid on the casserole, and place in a cool oven (300 °F, gas 2) for about $2\frac{1}{2}$ hours.

I have served this dish on a number of occasions but the most memorable was when I prepared it for a dinner party I gave for Sir Alexander Korda, at the time when he was my boss.

On my arrival home after filming all day, I was a little short of time, and immediately went to the kitchen to prepare the Chicken Paprika.

I put it straight into the oven, and then arranged the rest of the menu.

Dinner time came, I served all my guests, and then sat down at the table.

I was horrified to see them all turn red in the face; then they started to cough and choke, and some had tears pouring down their faces.

To my horror I found that I had used red cayenne pepper instead of paprika, and had liberally sprinkled it over the casserole.

My immediate reaction was to get my guests to sit with their tongues in their wine glasses until they felt a little better.

I then retired sheepishly to the kitchen to produce a hasty snack.

LARRY GELBART

Crab Foo Yong (Crab Omelette)

Very simple, this.

You need:

1 *pan*
1 *cooker*
3 *eggs*
6½ *oz tin crab*
6 *spring onions*
little cream
pepper
soy sauce
little Accent
oil

First, pre-heat the pan.

Don't ask me how I happen to know this, just put a small flame under the pan while you're screwing up the other ingredients, because it's always a good idea when preparing eggs for scrambling or omeletting or whatever.

While the pan is heating, turn on the kitchen radio and pray that Jimmy Young is not on.

With the radio at medium loud, open the tin of crab, drain all the water from it, then remove all the plastic-like bits from the crab (I don't know what they're called—how much does a nice, young Jewish boy know about crab altogether?) and put all the good stuff in a bowl.

Next, chop the onions very finely, all the way down the white part and the green, stopping just before you get to your fingernails.

Add these to the crab (the onions, not the nails).

Now, the eggs.

Crack them with one hand (like Audrey Hepburn in *Sabrina Fair;* not for better taste, its just more stylish), and drop them into the bowl.

Add a little cream and pepper.

No salt: add a bit of shoyu (or soy sauce), that's salty enough.

Stir eggs, crab and onions together.

Add a little Accent.

Drop enough oil on the pan to cover its now-hot surface, then empty the contents of the bowl and turn up the flame.

Lift the corners of the eggs (I assume you're using a square pan, otherwise lift the edges) once they begin to fry, and let the wet parts spread and touch the pan's surface.

Make the omelette wet or dry to taste.

If you don't like the result, I'll pay you back for everything but the cooker.

I hope this serves.

CRAB OMELETTE   ARTIST: HARRIET FREEDMAN

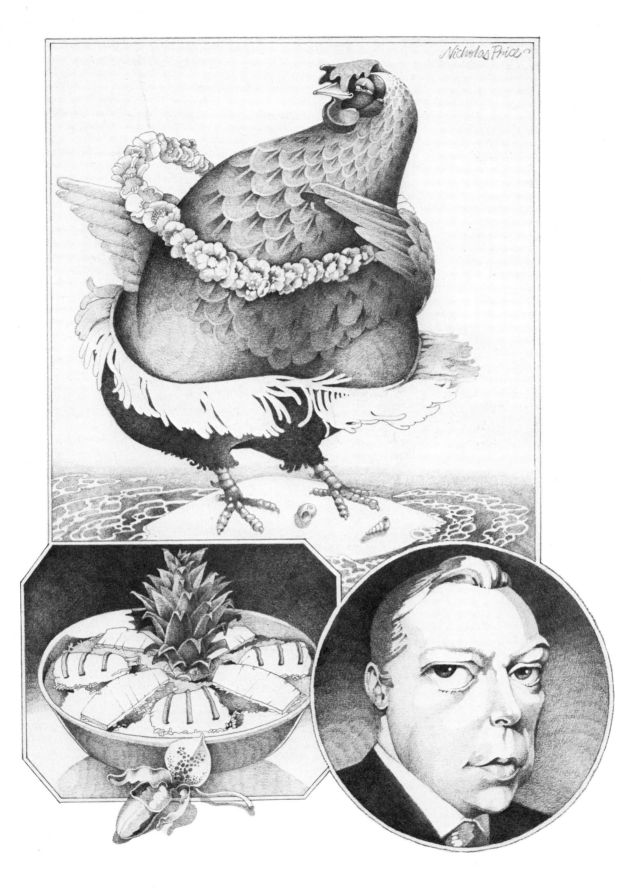

HERBERT LOM/HAWAIIAN CHICKEN   ILLUSTRATOR: NICHOLAS PRICE

HERBERT LOM

Hawaiian Chicken Rice

Serves 4

oil for frying
2 large onions
little garlic
1 chicken
salt and pepper
1 teaspoon ginger
8 oz long grain rice
4 oz chopped celery
1 tin bamboo shoots
1 small tin pineapple rings (or fresh pineapple if available)
1 pimiento
soy sauce
paprika

Heat the oil, chop the onions and a little garlic, and mix.

Cook gently until soft and tender.

Cut the chicken into four pieces (save bones etc for stock), boil in water for 2 hours, then pour 1½ pints stock into a dish, add salt and pepper, and ginger.

Boil and simmer for 30 minutes.

Add rice, celery, and bamboo shoots, and simmer for 15 minutes.

Garnish all round with leaves (from the celery, or broccoli etc).

Place on top pineapple rings laced with pimiento strips.

Perhaps add a little soy sauce and paprika.

Put an orchid in the middle, or perhaps a couple of carnations or roses will do!

Serve fresh, and wait for blue skies to appear outside your window.

When London skies are grey, it is raining outside my window and I feel the need to remind myself of some of the sunny places I have worked in recently, I invite a couple of friends and prepare Hawaiian Chicken and Rice—or is it Maoi Chicken?

(Maoi is a small Hawaiian island, nothing to do with Chairman Mao.)

It was prepared for me by a friend in Honolulu where pineapples and orchids and pretty girls grow.

133

LELIA GOLDONI

Chicken à la Goldoni

olive oil
1 chicken
½ lb mushrooms
3 tablespoons butter
paprika
1 teaspoon grated lemon rind
whole wheat or regular flour
1 pint stock
salt and pepper
2 oz natural yoghurt

Pour olive oil over the chicken and roast (300 °F, gas 2) for about 1½ hours depending on the size.

Sauté the sliced mushrooms in almost all the butter, adding a little paprika and grated lemon rind.

Add the remaining butter and enough flour to make a good stiff roux.

Add stock, salt and pepper to taste, and yoghurt.

Stir over a gentle heat until hot.

Carve the chicken and pour sauce over the pieces.

This is a marvellous recipe for busy actresses and those people who don't have much time for preparation.

It's delicious too.

Lelia Goldoni

LELIA GOLDONI   ILLUSTRATOR: GRAY JOLIFFE

OMELETTE AU BLÉ   ILLUSTRATOR: ENZO APICELLA

ANNIE ROSS
AND JIMMY LOGAN

Omelette au Blé

1 *tablespoon milk*
6 *eggs*
$\frac{1}{4}$ *lb Swiss chard*
2 *cloves of garlic*
2 *tablespoons butter*
$\frac{1}{4}$ *wedge of lemon*
salt and pepper

Beat the eggs with the milk.

Melt the butter in an omelette pan, when frothy, add Swiss chard.

Fry until chard wilts, then add crushed garlic.

Fry 1 minute more.

Add eggs and proceed as for an omelette.

Add salt and pepper to taste.

Turn out onto a plate and squeeze a wedge of lemon over the top.

DAVID FROST

Mignon de Veau Jacques-René

Serves 1

escalope of veal, preferably Dutch
salt and pepper
flour
butter
1 slice ham
5 asparagus tips (fresh when in season)
grated Cheddar or Gruyère cheese
1 tablespoon dry white wine

Season the escalope with a little salt and pepper, flour and cook very lightly in butter.

Put the escalope in an oven-proof dish, copper with lead if available.

On top of the escalope place the ham, asparagus tips, a little grated cheese, and a nut of butter.

Brown under the grill.

When golden, bring on top of the stove, and pour over the dry wine which has been boiled.

Serve quickly and very hot.

I always like to have tiny little French peas cooked in butter as an accompaniment.

This is a very good combination.

Over the past few years I must have eaten Mignon de Veau at Chez Solange at least one hundred times and like it so much I refuse to try anything else!

It is the most delicious dish imaginable—with the exception, of course, of the deviser of this book.

DAVID FROST   ILLUSTRATOR: MARC BOXER

A CHICKEN   PHOTOGRAPHER: JOHN LAWRENCE-JONES

EILEEN ATKINS

Supreme de Volaille Mangue

Serves 4

4 *fresh chicken breasts* (140 *g without skin*)
80 *g fresh mango* (*diced*)
10 *g flour*
2 *eggs*
50 *g desiccated coconut*
40 *g breadcrumbs*
50 *g butter*
200 *g carrots* (*sliced*)
200 *g courgettes* (*sliced*)
seasoning

Remove the fillets from the chicken breasts.

Split the breasts.

Flatten these and the fillets.

Fill the breasts with mango, lay the fillets on top and fold over ends and sides.

Panne with flour, eggwash breadcrumbs and coconut mix.

Fry in clarified butter and finish in the oven.

Garnish with carrots and courgettes, glazed.

Serve chicken breast on top of vegetables.

Anton Mosimann, the head chef at the Dorchester, lives upstairs and if I want to attempt anything showy but simple he helps me out. This is one of his.

DAVID ESSEX

Essex Curry

Serves 4

1 large onion
1½ lb minced beef
salt
black pepper
1 tablespoon paprika
curry powder (to your taste)
4 cloves of garlic (NOT optional)
6 large mushrooms (sliced)
1 large green pepper (sliced)
1 tube tomato purée
1 can white kidney beans (or anything else you fancy)

Fry onions and minced beef until brown; add salt and black pepper, paprika, curry powder and garlic.

Cook for a further few minutes adding mushrooms, green pepper and tomato purée.

Then cook for 20 minutes turning all the time.

Add the kidney beans and cook for a further 5 minutes.

Side Vegetables

2 oz butter
salt and pepper
tomato purée (as you like it)
1 teaspoon curry powder
½ teaspoon chili powder
2 cloves of garlic
4 boiled potatoes
1 small cauliflower (divided and boiled)

Melt butter in a frying pan, add salt, pepper, tomato purée, curry powder, chili powder and garlic.

Mix together and sauté the potatoes and cauliflower for about 10 minutes.

Serve with diced onion and cucumber in plain yoghurt and popadoms.

P.S. *Don't speak to anyone the next day!*

ESSEX CURRY   ILLUSTRATOR: ARTHUR ROBINS

SEAN CONNERY   ILLUSTRATOR: LARS HAAKONSSEN

SEAN CONNERY

Spiced Beef with Parsley Dumplings

4 lb roll pickled beef
1 large onion stuck with cloves
2 bay leaves
ground pepper and salt
2 tablespoons dry mustard
1 green cabbage

Order the beef from the butcher.

Put it into a large casserole pan, add onion, bay leaves, seasoning, and above all, the mustard.

Cut the cabbage into this, cover with water, and simmer gently for about 3 hours.

Remove the beef and keep hot, strain the broth the meat was cooked in, and return to the heat.

Drop in the dumplings (see below) from a wet spoon, cover, and leave to steam for 15–20 minutes.

PARSLEY DUMPLINGS

½ lb sifted flour
4 level teaspoons baking powder
1 teaspoon salt
4 tablespoons butter
2 beaten eggs
4 tablespoons finely chopped parsley
½ pint milk

Sieve together the dry ingredients, rub in the butter until the mixture is like fine breadcrumbs.

Gradually work in the eggs and milk, and finally, the parsley.

The beef slices beautifully, and is a lovely colour: serve it with broccoli.

It's elegant enough for a dinner party, yet substantial enough to please the men.

Sean Connery

145

GERALDO

Chicken Casserole

Serves 6

1 *large or 2 small chickens*
oil for frying
2 *large onions*
2 *bacon rashers*
1 *bouquet garni*
1 *sherry glass brandy*
1 *cup water*
salt and pepper
garlic
6 *oz mushrooms*
12 *small potatoes*
½ *tin petit pois*

Cut the chicken into 8 pieces.
In a heavy saucepan, fry the roughly chopped onions in the oil.

When light brown, add the chopped bacon and the chicken.
Do not salt the chicken in case the bacon is too salty.
Turn the chicken pieces now and then to colour them slightly (about 8 minutes), add the bouquet garni, and transfer to an oven-proof dish.
Add the brandy and water, cover and cook at 350 °F, gas 4, for about 30 minutes.
Add salt, pepper, and garlic to taste.
Peel and quarter the mushrooms.
Peel the potatoes.
Put into the casserole with the chicken, and cook for 15 minutes.
Add the peas, cook for a further 5 minutes, and then serve.

Red Cabbage

1 *large red cabbage, sliced finely*
1 *large onion, finely chopped*
oil for frying
4 *sugar lumps*
salt
2 *glasses cooking wine*
1 *grated apple*
2 *slices honey bread*

Fry onion until golden-brown.

Put into an oven-proof dish, add sugar, salt, apple, wine and bread, and cook at 350 °F, gas 4, for 2 hours, stirring occasionally.
If necessary, add water or wine.

The longer the cabbage is left to cook, the better it tastes.
Do not add too much liquid at a time, and serve dry.

Cabbage Salad

1 *large white cabbage, sliced finely*
1 *teaspoon caraway seeds*
little caster sugar
oil and vinegar
1 *large tablespoon mayonnaise*
1 *oz walnuts*

Put cabbage into a large dish, and salt; cover, and leave for 3 hours.
Remove the water which has col-

lected at the bottom, add the caraway seeds, a little sugar, oil, vinegar to taste, and finally the mayonnaise and the chopped walnuts.
Stand for 1 hour in the refrigerator before serving.

Bon appétit

GERALDO   ILLUSTRATOR: ARNOLD SCHWARTZMAN

FAY WELDON   PHOTOGRAPHER: MICHAEL BERKOFSKY

FAY WELDON

Quails

I won't give you my sugarless Christmas Pudding recipe.

I gave that to a women's magazine, once, and come Christmas Day, millions of steaming puddings emerged from millions of up-turned basins, bright green with mould . . . .

You will be safe, however, with the following quail recipe if only because these small plump birds are almost impossible to undercook, and over-cooking, in my frequent experience, doesn't do much damage.

Allow 2 quails per head for a main dish.

Stuff with grapes.

Season.

Brown in butter.

Transfer, juices and all, to a braising dish and over your quails pour a spoonful or so of either stock, cream or calvados.

If you wish to drape them with bacon and cook uncovered, by all means do, otherwise lay them on a mirepoix, a bed of mushrooms, or tinned red cabbage, and cover.

Cook for some 20 minutes (350 °F, gas 4).

Serve with creamed (and I mean creamed and not just squashed) potatoes and as much of the gravy as you can acquire, by adding more of the stock, cream or calvados you started with, or indeed all three.

Cowards will no doubt thicken with flour.

It all sounds extremely expensive and is.

Fay Weldon

BEVERLY & VIDAL SASSOON

Health Foods

cauliflower/cheese/apple
raw mushrooms (in lemon and oil)
cauliflower/pineapple
celery/apple
carrot/coconut
carrot/cheese/fruit
egg/onion
cabbage/cucumber/orange
cottage cheese/prunes
chicory/sweetcorn/apples
tomatoes/cucumber/cheese
cabbage/cheese/apple/nuts

All the vegetables should be finely chopped or grated, and bound with a little salad dressing made with oil, egg yolk, and lemon juice.

We usually serve a little of each on a thin bed of lettuce and sprinkle with some mixed ground nuts.

A meal consisting of some of these salads is very satisfying, and there is none of the heavy feeling one sometimes gets after a meal with meat and rich foods.

I have a feeling that Vidal first tried the real 'health' dinner at the White Elephant.

He used to creep around the corner from his old Curzon Street 'pad' and ask for a salad with everything but *everything* in it.

There are a million different combinations, but here are some that we tend to favour most.

More often than not our menu is one of health foods and a great variety of salads.

When we do have a 'hot' meal, there is one dish that Vidal enjoys and it is made in South America quite a lot.

Again thinking along the health food lines, we avoid frying and instead bake the chicken for 1 hour at 350 °F, gas 4.

However, before putting it in the oven, pour over the chicken or chicken pieces a fairly thick mixture of mustard, salt and pepper, water, and lemon juice.

The taste is fantastic.

Beverly & Vidal

VIDAL'S FORK   DESIGNER: NANCY FOUTS

Peter Le Vasseur 1972

RICHARD ATTENBOROUGH   ILLUSTRATOR: PETER LE VASSEUR

SHEILA & DICKIE ATTENBOROUGH

Rognons Sautés Turbigo

Serves 4

2 *oz butter*
4 *sheep kidneys*
¾ *lb chipolata sausages*
2 *dozen button onions*
4 *oz mushrooms*
salt and pepper
1 *teaspoon tomato purée*
1 *dessertspoon flour*
1 *wine glass white wine*
1 *tablespoon sherry*
¾ *pint stock*
2 *bay leaves*
2 *slices stale bread*
oil for frying
chopped parsley

Melt the butter in a sauté pan.
Skin the kidneys, cut in half, and remove the core.
Divide each sausage in two, and brown the kidneys and sausages slowly in the hot butter.
Remove them, and add blanched button onions, and mushrooms cut into four.
Season and cook for 5–6 minutes, stirring occasionally.

Then add tomato purée and flour.
Leave to brown a little.
Take off the heat, and add the wine, sherry and stock.
Return to the heat, and stir until it boils.
Replace the sausages and kidneys, and add the bay leaves.
Cover the pan with foil, put the lid on, and simmer gently on the heat for 20–25 minutes.

CROÛTONS

Cut the bread into rectangular pieces and fry in a little hot oil until golden-brown.
Serve the kidneys on a hot dish, surround with croûtons, and sprinkle the top with parsley.

The old boy adores kidneys and so this has been in my small repertoire as a favourite for some time!

I always eat far too much of this and suffer agony—but what divine agony!

153

RALPH THOMAS

Filets Mignons Flambés à la Jacques Coeur

1 *slice beef tenderloin per person (cut*
1½ inch thick)
1 *clove garlic*
salt and coarsely ground pepper
circles of bread, cut to the size of the filets
butter for frying
1 *teaspoon warmed brandy per filet*
watercress, grilled tomatoes, french fried
potatoes, to garnish

Rub the beef slices on both sides with garlic, and season generously.

Sauté the bread in plenty of butter until crisp and brown on both sides.

In a separate frying pan, cook the filets in hot butter over a high flame.

They should be brown, but rare inside.

Then slip a croûton under each filet, and add a little melted butter to the pan.

Pour in the brandy, light it, and shake the pan until the flame dies out.

Transfer the croûtons and filets to a large hot platter, pour on the pan juices, and garnish.

When Betty Box and I were shooting *A Tale of Two Cities* in Central France, it rained for six weeks solidly, and we used to sit in a little bistro called 'Jacques Coeur' in Bourges, praying for the sun.

The chef taught me several party pieces and I have had great success with this one.

I have set fire to the dining room curtains twice, but it seems to improve the flavour!

Do hurry up, dearest. Dinner's getting cold!

FILETS MIGNONS FLAMBES   ILLUSTRATOR: GRAY JOLIFFE

FISH PIE   DESIGNER: NANCY FOUTS (SHIRTSLEEVE STUDIO)

JOHN MORTIMER

The unwholesome and repellent food at school led me, in my schooldays, to cook omelettes according to Marcel Boulestin's instructions ('Always get the pan so hot that the almond-sized pat of butter jumps about when placed in it') over the study fire.

Since then I have cooked assiduously, and a major irritant for any lady who has ever lived with me has been that she is only grudgingly allowed into the kitchen.

I think that English food, properly understood, is by far the best in the world, and I have chosen the most resolutely dull English dish in my repertoire: in fact, it's delicious.

Fish pie fills everyone up, and allows you to talk to them without a constant dash from the room to save the flaming grill or the collapsing soufflé.

Cooking it has a remarkably soothing effect after a day at the Old Bailey, and many plots occur to you whilst peeling the potatoes.

Cook to the accompaniment of a private bottle of Sancerre and *Any Questions* on the radio.

This programme provides the element of frustrated loathing and rage which is missing in the dish itself.

Fish Pie

I have never bought a pair of scales so it's no good asking me how much of anything.

lots of cod or any white fish—ask the fish-monger to skin it
plenty of butter
flour
milk
7 eggs
1 small onion
fresh parsley
2 packets of prawns (frozen will do)
1 jar mussels
some potatoes
salt and pepper
grated cheese
breadcrumbs

Grill the fish—this is important as it gives far more flavour than steaming it.

Make a white sauce with the butter, flour and milk.

Hardboil 6 eggs, and add them (sliced with onion and chopped parsley) to the white sauce.

Add the fish when it's cooked, together with the prawns and mussels, and put the lot into a buttered oven-proof dish.

Now cream the potatoes over a low heat with a lot of butter and seasoning, break 1 egg into it, and stir.

Also add grated cheese to give flavour to the potatoes.

Make a cover for the fish with the potatoes, and sprinkle with bread-crumbs.

Cook in the oven at 350 °F, gas 4 until golden-brown.

Serve with hard white cabbage which you should cook with a lot of butter (add a cup of water only in the last few minutes), and red cabbage cooked in brown sugar, vinegar, and beer.

Open the other six bottles of Sancerre and turn off *Any Questions*.

[signature: John Mortimer]

ROGER MOORE

Fettucine alla Panna

Serves 4

½ *lb mushrooms*
1 *lb peas*
1½ *lb fettucine*
salt
½ *lb butter*
½ *pint double cream*
Parmesan cheese
ground black pepper

(Fettucine is a pasta but if not obtainable from delicatessens, the recipe can be made with ordinary spaghetti.)

Boil the mushrooms in water for 10 minutes, drain, and if large cut into quarters.

Cook peas and drain.

Boil the fettucine in salted water for 5 minutes.

Drain off surplus water and put immediately into a heated dish.

Melt the butter in a saucepan, and when hot add the mushrooms and peas.

Lightly whisk the cream and add to the butter mixture when it boils.

Bring back to just on the boil, then pour over the fettucine.

Mix thoroughly and grate fresh Parmesan cheese over the top; serve with ground black pepper.

Gnocchi de Patate

Serves 4

Boil 3 lb potatoes in their skins.
When cooked, drain and peel.

Sieve the hot potato onto a pastry board, and when cool, mix in sufficient flour to bind softly (just until it does not stick to the hands).

Cut into pieces, and roll each piece on a lightly floured board into a 1 inch thick roll.

Cut diagonally into 1 inch long pieces.

Bring a large saucepan of salted water to the boil, add potato pieces (gnocchi), and bring back to the boil. The gnocchi will rise, and when this happens, spoon out with a small sieve into a heated dish.

Serve with Parmesan cheese, and sauce of your own preference—mince, tomato or just melted butter.

ROGER MOORE   DESIGNER: LOU KLEIN

PETER FINCH

Georgian Lamb Casserole

Take some lamb cutlets, and cut away all the fat and bone, leaving just the rounds of lamb.

Chop leeks, spring onions, and spanish onions together.

Place the lamb in the bottom of a casserole, cover with the mixed onions and leeks, and just cover with a mixture of sweet white wine and a little beef stock.

Slice a lemon, removing the peel, and place the slices on top of the mixture.

Add a little grated lemon peel separately.

Cover and cook in a moderate oven (350 °F, gas 4) for about 2 hours.

LORD AND LADY DELFONT

Shepherd's Pie

Serves 4

1 *large onion*
1 *oz margarine*
2 *lb best lean minced beef*
1 *large tablespoon tomato purée*
1 *beef stock cube*
1 *teaspoon Marmite*
1 *teaspoon sugar*
2 *bay leaves*
1 *teaspoon basil*
1 *heaped tablespoon flour*
salt and pepper to taste
1 *cup milk*

Chop the onion and fry till soft in the margarine.

Remove from the pan, add the mince, and turn up heat.

Cook quickly, stirring all the time, for 10 minutes or until the meat is brown.

Add a little more margarine, if necessary.

Put back the onions, and add all the other ingredients except the milk.

Stir well, and when mixed, add milk slowly until the dish has a creamy consistency.

Put in an oven-proof dish, and allow to cool.

When set, add well seasoned mashed potatoes, and dot with butter.

Put in a hot oven (425 °F, gas 7) for about 45 minutes, or until top is crusty and brown.

I hope this turns out all right because I hardly ever measure anything.

The only thing one must be careful of is not to make it 'sloppy'.

It should turn out quite firm, and the potato should be crispy.

This is Bernie's favourite Saturday lunch.

He says it brings him luck when he watches racing on T.V. afterwards, although I must say I haven't noticed that.

Carole Delfont

I do enjoy my Shepherd's Pie each Saturday before racing but, of course, as is usual with husbands, I never tell my wife whether I have won or lost.

Bernie

SHEPHERD'S PIE   ILLUSTRATOR: SARA MIDDA

STANLEY MANN

Chicken Vindaloo

Serves 4

1 *medium-sized part-cooked chicken*
2 *large onions*
ghee or butter
1 *dessertspoon curry powder*
1 *teaspoon paprika*
1 *teaspoon cumin powder or seed*
1 *teaspoon cardomom*
salt and pepper
1 *green pepper*
chicken stock, if necessary
1 *large tin tomatoes*
¼ *lb creamed coconut*
rice ⎫
raisins ⎬ *as desired*
almonds ⎭
2 *bananas*
¾ *lb seedless or seeded grapes*

Chop and fry the onions in ghee or butter.

Add all the spices, salt and pepper, and cook gently for 3 minutes.

Add the chopped green pepper.

Remove chicken from the bone, and add to the spices with the juice from the tomatoes.

Cook for 5 minutes.

Add tomatoes and creamed coconut, cover partly and simmer gently for 1 hour.

Keep a little stock from the chicken to add if necessary.

Meantime, boil the rice, and when cooked fry in a little butter, then add raisins and chopped almonds.

Add the chopped banana and halved grapes 10 minutes before serving.

Stanley Mann

This recipe was originally taken from Georgia Brown some three years ago.

Georgia lost it herself and I know has been frantically searching for it ever since—so here it is, Georgia!

It is great for a party and equally good for a small group.

CHICKEN VINDALOO   ILLUSTRATOR: JOHN TRIBE

LYN & BARRY TOOK

Chump Chop Hot-Pot

Serves 4

4 thick chump chops
salt and pepper
flour
butter
1 lb carrots
2 medium-sized onions
½lb packet frozen peas
4 tomatoes
Worcester sauce
Tabasco
2 good pinches mixed herbs (not oregano!)

Coat the chops well in seasoned flour.

Put into a frying pan which contains melted butter, and brown well all over. Season again.

Put the chops into a casserole, and add raw sliced carrots, raw chopped onions and frozen peas.

Skin the tomatoes, cut in half, and add to the dish.

Add Worcester sauce (as strong as you like), Tabasco, and mixed herbs.

Add water until the liquid in the casserole just covers the ingredients.

Cover the casserole and put it in the oven at 225°F, gas ¼, and cook for at least 4 hours.

If necessary thicken the sauce before serving.

Serve with a seasonal salad on the side.

We like patavia or watercress and tomato.

When we think of the great meals we've had at the White Elephant, we naturally feel a bit shy about sending you what for me has always been a great 'after hard day in the Television Centre' supper (Barry).

We had thought of sending you Barry's invention, the London Weekend Special, 'breaking eggs without making an omelette'!

The great thing about Chump Chop Hot-Pot is that it can be left while Lyn comes to a telerecording, and it doesn't mean we have to have bacon and eggs after the show.

It's warm and delicious (Barry).

The longer you leave it in the oven the better (Lyn).

I tend to moan about the small bits of bone I find in it (Barry).

He'd find bone in a minute steak (Lyn).

With it, drink any medium priced claret.

Whether the show's gone well or badly, you feel good after Chump Chop Hot-Pot.

REG VARNEY

Steak & Kidney Pudding

The suet pastry part is, of course, standard.

To make enough for four Reg Varney-size helpings you need:—

1½ lb stewing steak
½ lb kidney
seasoned flour
3 medium-sized onions
¼ lb mushrooms
2 beef stock cubes

Grease a pudding basin and line it with suet pastry.

Cut steak and kidney into small pieces and dip each piece into the seasoned flour.

Fill the basin with layers of seasoned steak and kidney, slices of onions and mushrooms.

Make enough stock to cover the meat.

Then cover with a layer of suet pastry, wrap the basin in greaseproof paper and foil, and cook in the steamer for 5–6 hours.

Slimming diets are set aside for this dish—but what a lovely way to put on weight.

PUDDINGS & CAKES

SPIKE MILLIGAN

Spaghettini Dolce

*spaghettini (can be bought in Italy or in an
Italian shop in Soho)*
$\frac{1}{2}$ *pint double cream*
2 flat tablespoons caster sugar
2 tablespoons brandy

Cook the spaghettini in the normal
way but do not add salt.

Whip the double cream, add the
caster sugar and brandy.

Pour the sauce over the spaghettini
while still hot.

Serve as a sweet.

Spike Milligan

RINALDO (MANAGER) & LESLIE CROWTHER   PHOTOGRAPHER: PETER HOWE

LESLIE CROWTHER

Portuguese Bread Mountain

½ lb white bread
½ pint red wine
14 oz caster sugar
½ teaspoon cinnamon
rind of ½ lemon, thinly peeled
3 eggs
fat for frying
apricot jam

Cut the bread into fingers, and put in a bowl.

Put the wine, 8 oz caster sugar, cinnamon and lemon rind into a small pan, and bring slowly to the boil.

Beat the egg yolks over heat until thick, and add the wine mixture, stirring all the time.

Strain over the bread fingers and leave for about 15 minutes.

Drain the bread fingers and fry in hot fat.

When cool, spread with jam and pile onto an oven-proof dish.

Make a meringue with the egg whites and remaining caster sugar, reserving a little sugar to sprinkle over the top.

Bake in a warm oven (325 °F, gas 3) until golden-brown.

The great thing about this dish, as a dessert, is that you economise on the brandy and liqueurs.

Two helpings of Portuguese Bread Mountain, and everybody is practically anybody's.

Three helpings and it's 'quickly nurse, the screens!!'

I don't know why half a pint of red plonk should be so potent when mixed with apricot jam etc, but it is.

I don't know much about Portuguese food, but if the Mountain is typical, then I can't wait to try the rest of the Range.

After which excruciating pun, the only thing to do is have another helping and forget I ever said it.

The best time to describe food is when you're tasting it—yes, darling, I will have a little more—talk amongst yourselves for a moment—and it really is worth tasting.

Buenos Nosh!

173

DOREEN & JACK HAWKINS

Beverly Hills Cheese Cake

$\frac{1}{2}$ *lb Dad's cookies and ginger snaps*
$\frac{1}{4}$ *lb butter, melted*
3 large packets Philadelphia cream cheese (each 3 oz)
$\frac{3}{4}$ *cup,* plus 1 tablespoon sugar*
1 teaspoon vanilla flavouring
2 eggs
1 pint sour cream

Crumble the cookies and ginger snaps, and mix with melted butter.

Press in spring form pan, about 9 inches in diameter.

Cream the cheese well with $\frac{3}{4}$ cup sugar.

Add $\frac{1}{2}$ teaspoonful vanilla and the eggs, one at a time.

Mix well.

Bake for 20 minutes at 350 °F, gas 4, then cool for about 30 minutes.

Put on topping of sour cream mixed with remaining sugar and vanilla.

Sprinkle the top with cookie crumbs.

Bake for 5 minutes in a hot oven (500 °F, gas 10).

Let the cake cool, and put in the refrigerator overnight.

Here is one of our favourite recipes that I managed to extract from a cook at the Beverly Hills Hotel in California.

I have used it many times with enormous success and can assure you that it does work!

Like coals to Newcastle!

My wife invariably serves it to our American friends—their praise is positively drooling.

* *1 cup = 8 fl oz*

Doreen

Jack Hawkins

174

JACK HAWKINS   ILLUSTRATOR: VICKY

MISS PIGGY

Kissy Kissy everyone.

As you might guess, one of my favourite pastimes is preparing a gay romantic dinner for two.

And you can guess who those two are, hmmm?

In fact, over the years moi have trained Kermit to be something of a gourmet.

When I first met my little green ball of passion his favourite dish was Dragonfly Tettrazini.

Note from Kermit: This is not true at all. In fact it was the other way round. When I first met Miss Piggy her favourite dish was Swill Almondine.

Now between performances when I am in the kitchen, I am *always* very calorie conscious.

Well, I just have to be.

I'm sure you can see that.

I mean, I just *must*!

Kermy has a tendency to put on weight.

So I am always searching for tempting sweets to eat after a meal that won't also add inches to the waistline. Here is one of your superstar's favourites.

Fraises Eau Distille

1 *itsy-bitsy basket fully ripe strawberries*
¼ *pint (approx.) distilled water*

Slice the berries thinly and arrange artistically in a silver bowl.

Add distilled water just to cover and allow to marinate for 2 hours before serving.

(Be certain to use only the finest distilled water available.)

Vous will be amazed at how the water brings out the flavour of the berries.

Incidentally, if your diet allows it, this recipe can be further improved by the addition of a teensy amount of caster sugar—say one-half to three-quarter's teaspoon.

On one or two truly festive occasions I have also sprinkled the berries with a dessertspoon of brandy, just before serving.

I do think, though, that if one is going to use the brandy, one should also add just a dollop of whipped cream on top, for culinary balance, you know.

And of course a delicate way to serve this delicious but slimming dessert is piled atop a good chocolate gateau filled with Bavarian cream, bananas, and slivered almonds!

Also, because one has been so good about watching those mean old calories, I always feel this dish can be served with a few little extras ... like maybe a half pound of rum-chocolate truffles and a few glasses of Benedictine!!!! ... Wonderful!

How about we top the whole thing with two or three scoops of vanilla ice cream or chocolate sauce.

(Many slimmers deny themselves unnecessarily. Did you know that a cup of chocolate sauce has fewer calories in it than a roast ox?)

Note from Kermit: I do not believe this was meant to be the end of the recipe. Piggy broke off writing quite suddenly, bolting for the door when she saw a McVities truck drive by the window. She'll return in 4 or 5 hours, her breath smelling of Jaffa Cakes, and be remorseful the rest of the day.

WRITER: JERRY JUHL

© HENSON ASSOCIATES, INC., 1979

MISS PIGGY   ARTIST: BRUCE MCNALLY

GLENDA JACKSON

Rum & Banana

Serves 4

6 *bananas*
3 *tablespoons demerara sugar*
juice of 1 *lemon*
3 *tablespoons water*
1 *sherry-glass rum*
cream

Peel the bananas, and put in an oven-proof dish.

Sprinkle with sugar, and add lemon juice and water.

Bake for about 35 minutes, until brown, at 325 °F, gas 3, adding the rum after about 15 minutes in the oven.

Serve with as much cream as you like.

This recipe is very simple to do, and is a great favourite of ours.

Glenda.

ALISTAIR COOKE

Ricotta Layer Cake

This is one of the most delicious desserts in the world and, as my wife has demonstrated many times, it is childishly easy to make.

1½ lb ricotta cheese
3 squares semi-sweet grated chocolate
almond flavouring
1 double layer sponge cake
icing sugar
1 egg white, whisked
1 tablespoon lemon juice

Thoroughly mix together the ricotta, 2½ squares of the grated chocolate, and almond flavouring to taste.

Slice each layer of the sponge cake in half, and fill the 3 intervals with the ricotta mixture. Mix as much icing sugar as you can into the egg white, add lemon juice and almond flavouring and work to the consistency of heavy cream.

Ice the sides and top of the cake.

Sprinkle the top with what is left of the grated chocolate.

This cake is noticeably better if it is made a day ahead and kept in the refrigerator.

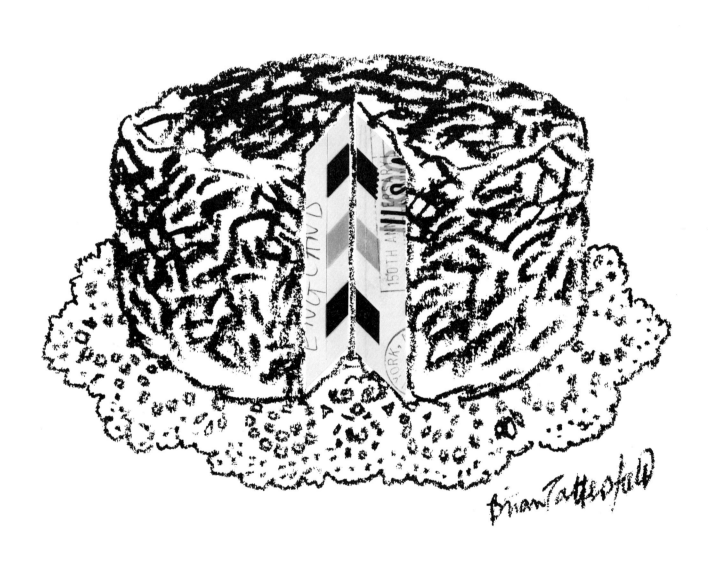

RICOTTA LAYER CAKE   ILLUSTRATOR: BRIAN TATTERSFIELD

Potato Scones

8 *oz boiled potato*
1 *dessertspoon warm milk*
1 *level teaspoon salt*
1½ *oz margarine*
2 *oz plain flour*

Mash the hot potato with the milk, salt, and margarine: beat until smooth.
Add flour to form a stiff dough.
Roll out to about ¼ inch.
Cut into rounds.
Bake in a hot oven (425 °F, gas 7) for about 10 minutes.
Serve with butter.

Easy Fruit Cake

12 *oz mixed fruit*
4 *oz sugar*
4 *oz butter (or margarine)*
¼ *pint water*
1 *beaten egg*
8 *oz self-raising flour*

Put the fruit, sugar, butter, and water into a saucepan.
Simmer slowly for 20 minutes, and allow to cool.
Add the egg and stir in the flour.
Bake in a greased 6 inch tin in a warm oven (325 °F, gas 3) for 1½ hours.

I have to confess that these two recipes are from my mother-in-law who is a super cook.

My culinary arts are a bit restricted and usually based around a big clove of garlic!!

Diana & Alan Lake.

HARRY SECOMBE

Welsh Cakes

$\frac{1}{4}$ *lb lard*
$\frac{1}{4}$ *lb butter*
1 *lb self-raising flour*
pinch of salt
4 *oz caster sugar*
3 *oz currants*
3 *oz sultanas*
2 *eggs, beaten*

Rub the fat into the flour, add the salt, sugar, and fruit, and make a well in the mixture.

Add the beaten eggs, and a little warm water if necessary.

Turn onto a floured board and knead lightly.

Roll the mixture out to $\frac{1}{2}$ inch thickness and cut out with a round fluted cutter.

Place the rounds on greased hotplate or griddle over a moderate heat, and cook on either—or rather, each!—side until golden-brown.

Welsh Cakes are a great favourite in our household—they don't do our waistlines any favours, but they certainly are delicious!

Harry Secombe

LESLIE PHILLIPS

Crème Brûlée

Mix ½ pint milk, ½ pint cream, and 1 oz sugar.

Add the grated rind of ½ lemon.

Add this mixture to 1 whole egg beaten with 4 egg yolks.

Beat well, and add 1 bay leaf.

Put mixture into an oven-proof dish set in a roasting tray half filled with water, and bake at 300 °F, gas 2 for 1¼ hours, or until set.

Remove from the oven, and allow to cool.

Then sprinkle the top with 6 oz demerara sugar, and place under a very hot grill until the caramel is glazed and brown.

It's very funny watching people struggle with the caramel as they get it stuck in their teeth!

Leslie Phillips

TONY RANDALL

Strawberries with Vinegar & Pepper

You must have the little wild strawberries, fraises du bois—no other kind will do.

Put them in a bowl and sugar them well.

Rotate them until the sugar is stained.

Then add a little champagne vinegar —no other kind.

Rotate some more.

Add some finely ground black pepper, not too much, not too little.

More rotating.

Sensational.

This is my favourite dessert and it's out of this world.

Tony Randall

TONY RANDALL/STRAWBERRY DESSERT   ILLUSTRATOR: ALAN CRACKNELL

RONNIE BARKER/GRAPE SPECIAL   PHOTOGRAPHER: ALAN BOYD

RONNIE BARKER

Grape Special

Serves 4

1 *lb seedless grapes*
½ *pint double cream*
large block vanilla ice cream
soft brown sugar

Put grapes into an oven-proof dish and pour cream over them.

Leave overnight in the fridge.

Just before serving, spread ice cream thickly over grapes and cream and then cover with a layer of brown sugar, making sure all the ice cream is covered.

Put under a very hot grill until sugar melts. Serve immediately.

This is my favourite way of grappling with the grape, and is far less dangerous than waiting until it has been liquidized and labelled.

Agamenis, the Greek confused poet (762–691 B.C.) said, 'He who follows the grape must make sure he does not overtake it before he is past it, for fear of it catching up with him.'

MORDECAI RICHLER

Noah's Apple Cake

1 *cup* butter*
1½ *cups* sugar*
3 *cups* sifted bread flour*
4 *teaspoons baking powder*
1 *teaspoon salt*
4 *beaten eggs*
2 *teaspoons vanilla*

Cream the butter well, blending it gradually with the sugar.

Cut in the flour so that the mixture resembles fine breadcrumbs.

Do not allow it to become heavy.

Reserve ¾ cup of this mixture.

To the rest, add the baking powder, salt, eggs diluted in 6 tablespoons water, and vanilla.

Spread half the mixture in a greased and floured shallow pan approximately 9 × 13 inches.

Add the apple filling, cover with the remaining half of the paste and, finally, sprinkle the reserved mixture on top.

Bake the cake for approximately 1 hour in a pre-heated oven (350 °F, gas 4).

FILLING

Peel, core, and slice 6 large well-flavoured apples, preferably Bramleys, and toss with ¼ cup raisins, ¼ cup desiccated coconut, ¼ cup sugar, 1 teaspoon cinnamon.

*1 cup = 8 fl oz

NOAH'S APPLE CAKE ILLUSTRATOR: TONY MEEUWISSEN

NANETTE NEWMAN & BRYAN FORBES

Peaches in Brandy

Serves 4

4 firm ripe peaches
1 cup water
few cloves
butter
1 teaspoon powdered mace
½ cup granulated sugar
brandy

Plunge the peaches into boiling water for a few seconds, then remove the skins.

Stick with a few cloves.

Place in oven-proof dish, dot with butter, sprinkle with mace and sugar.

Cover the dish.

Cook until just tender.

Add brandy (as much as you like).

Serve hot or cold with thick cream.

This is the ideal food to celebrate the end of a diet.

The only disadvantage I have found is that Nanette always uses my best brandy.

TWIGGY & JUSTIN   PHOTOGRAPHER: BARRY LATEGAN, DESIGN: SHIRTSLEEVE

TWIGGY & JUSTIN

Traditional English Christmas Pudding

1 cup hot milk
1 cup dry breadcrumbs
½ cup sugar
4 egg yolks, well beaten
½ lb seeded raisins, cut in pieces and floured
¼ lb figs, chopped
2 oz citron, cut fine
½ lb suet, chopped
¼ cup wine, grape juice or currant jelly
1 teaspoon nutmeg
¾ teaspoon cinnamon
¼ teaspoon clove
¼ teaspoon mace
1½ teaspoons salt

Put the milk and breadcrumbs in a bowl, and let them stand until cool.

Then add the sugar, egg yolks, raisins, figs, and citron.

Work with fingers or a wooden spoon until creamy.

Add the suet, and stir in the wine, nutmeg, cinnamon, clove, mace, and salt.

Beat the egg whites until stiff, and stir the mixture well.

Don't forget to add the real English sixpences, then steam.

To steam:
Butter a pudding mould.
Fill not more than ⅔ full to allow for expansion.
Put on cover or cover tightly with cooking foil.

Set the filled mould on a rack in a pan.

Add boiling water until it comes ½ way up the mould.

Cover tightly.

Adjust the heat to keep the water boiling throughout the steaming, adding more as it boils away, and steam for 6 hours.

Set the mould in cold water for a few seconds.

Uncover and turn out.

If you like fruit puddings less moist, set in the oven for a few minutes to dry out.

Serve with hot custard sauce and decorate with holly leaves.

193

LORD AND LADY GRADE

Lew's Christmas/Birthday Cake

$\frac{1}{4}$ lb butter
$\frac{1}{4}$ lb soft brown sugar
1 oz Bourneville chocolate block
1 lb plain flour
1 tsp cinnamon
1 tsp mixed spice
$\frac{1}{4}$ tsp nutmeg
3 eggs
6 oz mixed peel
$\frac{1}{4}$ lb glacé cherries
$\frac{1}{2}$ lb currants
$\frac{1}{2}$ lb raisins
$\frac{1}{2}$ lb sultanas
1 small tin of strawberries
1 tsp lemon juice
sherry or whisky to mix
$\frac{1}{4}$ lb whole almonds for decoration

Cream the butter and sugar together.
Melt the chocolate and add to this mixture.
Leave to one side.
Sieve the flour and spices and divide into three parts.
Add yolks of eggs to creamed mixture with the first part of the flour.
Beat egg whites stiffly and fold into the creamed mixture adding the second part of the flour.

Add the third part of the flour with the dried fruit to the mixture.
Drain the strawberries.
Add them with the lemon juice and spirit to the mixture by folding.
Line an 8 inch cake tin with several layers of brown paper around the outside of the tin to stop the cake from burning on the outside.
Put the mixture in the lined tin.
The almonds go on top as you wish.
Bake in a pre-heated oven on 275 °F, gas 1 for $\frac{1}{2}$ an hour and turn down to 240 °F, gas $\frac{1}{2}$ for 2–2$\frac{1}{2}$ hours.
Decorate as you wish for a Christmas cake but I always decorate it as a surprise birthday cake for Lew as he was born on Christmas Day.

Kathy Grade,

I should not eat it, but I love it

Lew Grade.

194

LORD GRADE   ILLUSTRATOR: PAT GAVIN

POMPEII PUDDING   ILLUSTRATOR: MEL CALMAN

FRANKIE HOWERD

Pompeii Pudding

3 *eggs, separated*
1 *pint milk and cream, mixed*
lemon rind
4 *oz breadcrumbs*
4 *tablespoons raspberry jam*
2 *oz caster sugar*

Beat the egg yolks and add the warmed milk, cream, and lemon rind.

Mix in the breadcrumbs.

Put jam into greased soufflé dish, spreading it over the bottom.

Pour milk mixture over this, and put aside for 30 minutes.

Bake in a cool oven for 1 hour (275 °F, gas 1).

Whip egg whites until stiff, then fold in sugar.

Pile on top of baked custard, sprinkle with sugar, and put into a cool oven (250 °F, gas ½) until set and very lightly browned.

What with all this dieting, it is considered almost criminal to eat sweet stuff these days but for us criminals who do—this is ideal!

RITA & THEODORE BIKEL

Ice Cream Caprice

Each time some temple sisterhood asks me for a recipe I have to quickly run to Theo and ask, 'may I send them the stuffed shrimp recipe', and he weeps, mutters something in the unknown tongue, and strikes his breast repeatedly.

Starting from there I cannot send you my terrific veal and milk recipe, or the shrimp glop recipe, or the spinach, bacon and cheese soufflé that Theo likes.

So here is a simple recipe for a dessert that has within it no religiously conflicting ingredients.

There is a restaurant on an island off San Francisco in Tiberon called the 'Caprice'.

It rests on strong poles set well into the water and looks out at the Golden Gate Bridge and the harbour lights of San Francisco.

At night it is gently breath-taking.

We have been told that gourmets, gourmands, and gluttons like ourselves, come from all over the world to sample the food and the wines from its superb cellars.

At the end of a fabulous dinner we had a simple dessert.

vanilla ice cream (as expensive as you can buy, please)
coffee beans (mixture of French and mocha)
coffee bean grinder (essential—who would want to eat tinned coffee grounds?)
brandy (French and as expensive as you are willing to sacrifice to these other ingredients)

Sprinkle freshly ground coffee over mounds of ice cream and reward the mixture with brandy (Courvoisier).

If you are sylphlike, unlike the rest of the world, you may add some marrons glacés, and munch on some meringues as well.

ICE CREAM CAPRICE   ILLUSTRATOR: IAN BECK

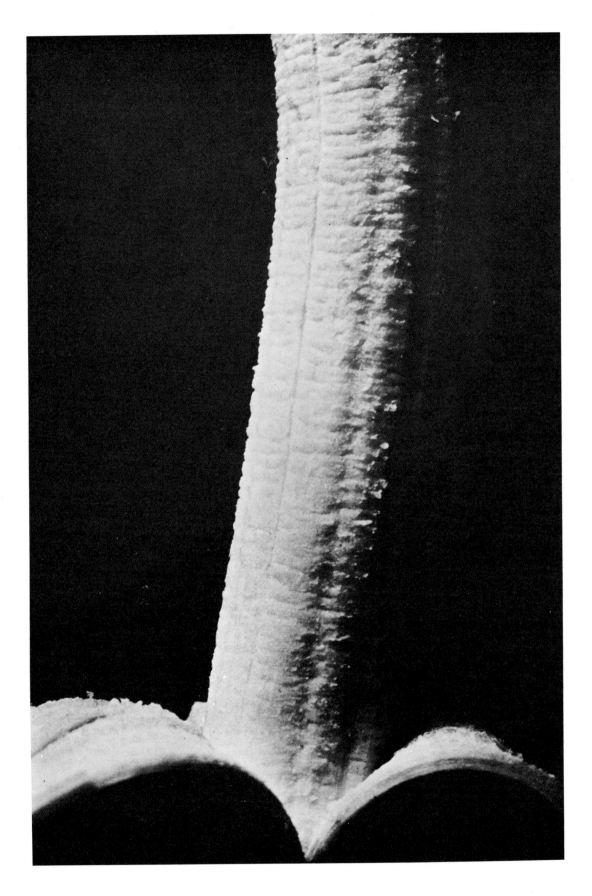

BANANA SPECIAL   PHOTOGRAPHER: HARRI PECCINOTTI

BILL WARD

Banana Flambé

8 ripe bananas
butter
caster sugar ⎫
brandy ⎬ *to taste*
whipped cream ⎭

Place the bananas in a buttered dish.

On top of each banana place a large walnut of butter.

Dust with sugar.

Place in a fairly hot oven (400 °F, gas 6) for about 7 minutes until soft, turning frequently.

Warm the brandy and pour over the bananas.

Set alight just before serving.

Serve with lashings of chilled whipped cream.

I suppose my interest in cooking started when I stopped actively producing and directing.

The need to create and obtain some kind of acclaim, criticism even, from an audience, however small, was still apparently present, demanding recognition.

Whatever the need, the satisfaction and joy obtained more than compensated for the occasional affectionate but severe reprimand from my wife about the state of the kitchen after I'd finished.

EDNA O'BRIEN

Miracle Cake

Make a sponge cake; that is, take 4 eggs, 4 oz caster sugar, and 4 oz white flour plus a pinch of salt.

Beat the eggs and sugar with a hand beater until such time as the figure 8 remains when sketched in the mixture.

Add the sieved flour intrepidly.

Put into a greased cake tin and bake in a hot oven (425 °F, gas 7) for 12 minutes.

Meanwhile, mash 1 banana, add 1 tablespoon lemon juice, and 1 oz caster sugar.

Slice some strawberries very thinly, and add a little orange juice.

Whip $\frac{1}{2}$ pint double cream and add a little cointreau.

When the cake is cool, cut it into two layers.

Put a coating of home-made raspberry jam on the bottom layer, then the banana, and one third of the cream.

Press the other layer on top, add the strawberries and the rest of the cream.

Allow a little time for the mixtures to soak through the sponges, then eat it, and enjoy it.

I have just made this and know it works!

LESLIE GRADE

Poires Belle Anita

Serves 6

6 firm ripe pears
vanilla essence
½ pint double cream
caster sugar
1 teaspoon kirsch
vanilla ice cream

Peel the pears leaving them whole and with the stalks, then poach for a few minutes in slightly sweetened, vanilla flavoured water.

Let them cool on a grill.

Whip the cream with a little sugar and kirsch.

Place the cool pears in a circle on a dish.

Pile ice cream in the middle, and coat the pears with the whipped cream.

If made in individual dishes, place the pear on a bed of ice cream, and coat with cream.

I can assure you this is a very nice dessert as I usually have to suffer it once a week and I cannot have any sugar or ice cream!

Chocolate Biscuit Pudding

Serves 6-8

8 oz bitter dessert chocolate
½ lb unsalted butter
3 oz caster sugar
2 eggs
½ lb digestive biscuits (well crushed)
2-3 oz chopped walnuts (or almonds)
grated peel of ½ orange
2 tablespoons brandy

Melt butter and chocolate. Beat eggs and sugar till fluffy;
slowly add melted chocolate and butter to egg mixture.
Stir in the crushed biscuit, grated orange peel, nuts and brandy
and put in a well-buttered bowl.
Refrigerate, and serve with cream.

It is very simple, absolutely delicious and a
marvelous way of playing hookey from weight watchers.

THE RT. HON. JOHN FREEMAN   Designer David Holmes

BITS & PIECES

JAMES MASON

Here is a jam recipe which my wife has given me for *The White Elephant Cook Book* :—

Plum Jam

6 *lb yellow plums*
6 *lemons*
8 *oz ginger in syrup*
6 *lb sugar*
$\frac{1}{4}$—$\frac{1}{2}$ *pint water*
3 *teaspoons ground ginger*
pectin, if desired

Wash and stone the plums.
Wash and slice the lemons finely.
Slice the ginger finely, and place in large pot.
Add the sugar and water, and bring to the boil over a medium heat.
Cook, stirring constantly, until the fruit becomes soft.
Add the ground ginger, and continue cooking for 5 minutes.
Add enough pectin for weight of fruit if desired, and continue cooking for a few more minutes.
Bottle in sterilized jars, and cover.

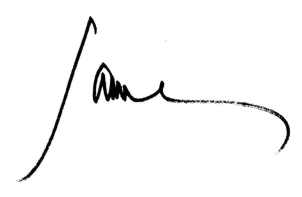

JANSSON'S TEMPTATION   ILLUSTRATOR: STEWART McKINNEN

DENIS NORDEN

Where cooking is concerned, I line up alongside Montaigne. 'Give me the provisions and the whole apparatus of a kitchen, and I would starve.'

In other words, I can only barely work out how to make orange juice.

So the ensuing recommendation is passed along without any kind of maker's guarantee.

The only personal involvement I have with its creation is that I once tasted it.

And it's smashing.

Mind you, I ate it under, as they say, ideal circumstances.

At the end of a disgraceful night just outside Stockholm.

The Swedes called it 'Jansson's Temptation'.

I never found out why.

When I asked who Jansson was and what was it he was tempted toward, they suddenly got very Scandinavian: came over all reticent and thin-lipped, and edged towards the sauna.

But, for me, it remains a perfect five-o'clock-in-the-morning dish for the terminal stages of a very good party.

Fattening, of course, with all the potatoes and cream—but that time of the morning, you should worry.

One last technical point.

The Swedish anchovy fillets have got to be Swedish ones.

Those tinned anchovies we get over here seem to be a quite different fish.

So ask around Soho, that's fun too.

Jansson's Temptation

Serves 4 healthy drunks

4 *cups raw potatoes*
1 *cup sliced onions*
⅓ *cup butter*
1 *tin Swedish anchovy fillets (remember— they must be Swedish!)*
1 *cup cream*

Cut the peeled potatoes into thin strips.

Sauté the onions in 2 tablespoons butter.

Butter a 1½ quart baking dish, and make a layer with half the potatoes.

Spread over this the anchovy fillets and the onions.

(Don't throw away the tin.)

Now put the remaining potatoes over as a top layer.

Take the juice from the tin of anchovies and sprinkle it all over.

Dot the remaining butter round the top, add half the cream and cover with foil.

Bake in a fairly hot oven (400 °F, gas 6) for 30 minutes.

Take off the foil, add the rest of the cream, and bake for another 20–30 minutes, until the potatoes are golden-brown.

Serve piping hot from the baking dish.

Denis Norden

HERMIONE GINGOLD

Quick Spaghetti Sauce

A wonderful quick sauce for spaghetti or practically anything.

Put 2 ounces of butter or margarine in a saucepan and melt slowly.

Add 2 or 3 cups* of water and stir in a packet of Lipton's Onion Soup (any make will do quite well).

Salt and pepper to taste and add 3 tablespoons of Heinz tomato ketchup and stir.

If you are feeding more than two you'll have to work out the quantities for yourself.

But remember two's company ...

Hermione Gingold

* 1 cup = 8 fl oz.

HERMIONE GINGOLD   ILLUSTRATOR: SEYMOUR CHWAST

Dear Stella,

I kept this as simple as I possibly can, but perhaps you
wanted something more complex. Do let me know if you
already have dozens of ham sandwiches.

See you in January,
All good wishes, as ever,

Len.
Len

Cooking - particularly French cooking - relies upon system,
and "creative" cooking is no part of my diet. There are however
dishes that benefit from being adapted and modified according
to the tastes of individuals. The croque-monsieur appears in
so many versions that very few cookery books attempt to define
it. So I make no apologies for the changes I have made to the
original, for that original was some other cook's modification.

CROQUE-MONSIEUR

Serves 1

1 slice bread (pain Anglais, not French loaf)
1 beaten egg
butter for frying
1 slice ham
1 slice Gruyère or Emmenthal cheese

Soak bread slice in well-beaten egg for 5 minutes. Fry
gently in the melted butter on both sides but don't cook it
right through or make it crisp. Upon the bread slice
put first the ham and then the cheese. Grill until the
surface of the cheese is browned and bubbling. Serve.

The result will vary according to the thickness of the ham, cheese
and bread. All of these items should be about the same shape.
A trace of garlic or mustard can be put between the cheese and
the ham. The result can be garnished with chopped chives or
chopped parsley.

LEN DEIGHTON   DESIGNER: DAVID PELHAM

WOLF MANKOWITZ

Spiced Hamburgers

Makes 10–12 hamburgers

1 *medium-sized onion*
1 *lb minced beef*
1 *lb minced pork or veal*
1 *egg*
1 *teaspoon ground cumin seed*
1 *teaspoon ground allspice (not mixed spice)*
salt and freshly ground pepper
cornflour or medium matzo-meal
oil for frying

Chop the onion into small pieces.
Mix all the other ingredients together except the cornflour and oil.
Form into hamburgers. Roll each one in cornflour or matzo-meal.
Fry in a little oil, or grill without fat.

Without doubt this is the world's greatest hamburger recipe!
It has the touch of the *kosher* which every Elephant hamburger really needs!

CORNISH PASTY   ILLUSTRATOR: JOHN TRIBE

WINSTON GRAHAM

A Cornish Pasty

Makes 1 pasty

rough puff pastry
6 oz skirt beef
1 oz ox kidney
2 medium-sized potatoes, peeled
1 onion
milk
salt and pepper

Roll the pastry into a circle.
We use a plate 8 inch in diameter!
Slice the potatoes very thinly onto the pastry, but not too near the edge.
Cut the meat very fine, and put on top of potatoes.
Then the kidney, also cut fine.
Slice the onion, varying amount to the tastes of your family.
Add salt and pepper.
Damp the edges of the pastry and 'crinkle' together.
Brush over with milk.
Place on greaseproof paper on a tin.
Bake at 450 °F, gas 8 for 20 minutes in the top of the oven, then put it (or them) on a lower shelf and cook for at least another 30 minutes.
Wrap in foil to keep hot, and eat with mustard.
Drink beer or a light wine.

We have made these for many of our friends both English and American.
They have eaten every bit and have not complained of indigestion!
Bad for slimmers but ideal for a picnic!

Winston Graham

GAYLE HUNNICUTT

Poppy Seed Dressing

The recipe as given will make $3\frac{1}{2}$ cups.

1 $\frac{1}{2}$ cups* sugar
2 teaspoons dry mustard
2 teaspoons salt
$\frac{2}{3}$ cup* vinegar
3 tablespoons onion juice
2 cups* salad oil (never olive oil)
3 tablespoons poppy seeds

Mix the sugar, mustard, salt, and vinegar. Add the onion juice, and stir in thoroughly.

Add the oil slowly, beating constantly, and continue to beat until thick.

Add the poppy seeds, and beat for a few minutes.

Store in a cool place or refrigerator.

This dressing is most easily mixed by a blender at a medium speed, but can be done by electric mixer or rotary beater (an endurance test!)

My personal touch is cutting down a bit on the sugar and adding garlic.

Being from Texas, I decided that the best contribution I could make from our family kitchen is a dressing recipe that's pure south.

It originated at the hands of Helen Corbitt who is renowned as the food director at Neiman-Marcus where it is served with fruit salads, green salads, avocado pears, shredded red cabbage, iced grapes—and it is delicious!

* 1 cup = 8 fl oz

Gayle Hunnicutt

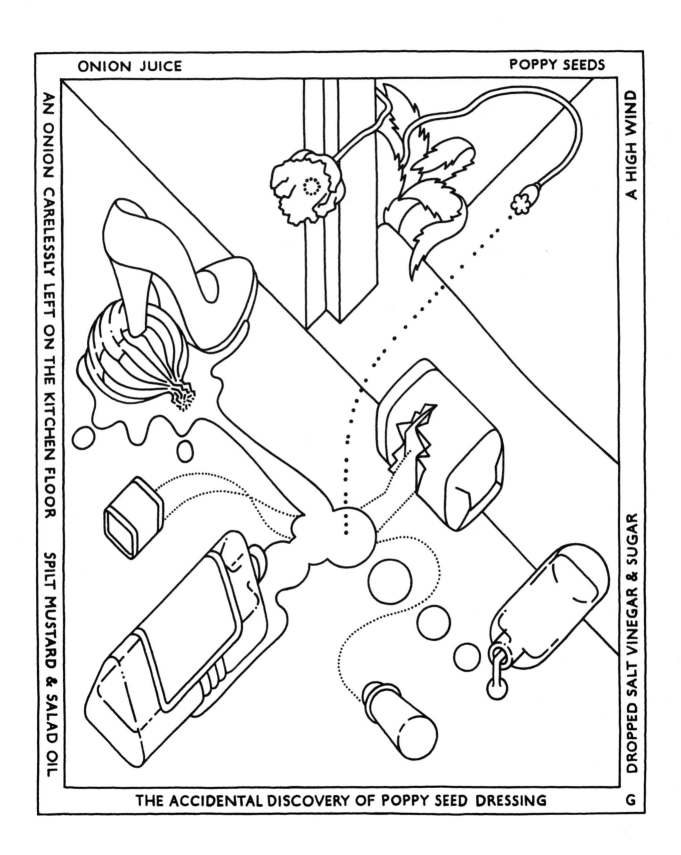

POPPY SEED DRESSING   ILLUSTRATOR: GEORGE HARDIE

BULL SHOT

·by·

JOHN OSBORNE

INGREDIENTS

VODKA	BLACK PEPPER
CANNED CONSOMME (UNDILUTED)	
TABASCO	LEMON JUICE

· DIRECTIONS ·

PUT THE INGREDIENTS (IN WHATEVER PROPORTIONS YOU CAN TAKE) INTO A COCKTAIL SHAKER AND SHAKE VIGOROUSLY.

YOU MAY NOT BE ABLE TO EAT IT WITH A KNIFE AND FORK BUT IT SHOULD CERTAINLY SET YOU UP **JOHN OSBORNE**

DESIGNED BY JOHN McCONNELL

JOHN OSBORNE/BULL SHOT   DESIGNER: JOHN McCONNELL

JOHN OSBORNE

Bull Shot

vodka
canned consommé (undiluted)
lemon juice
Tabasco
black pepper

Put the ingredients (in whatever proportions you can take) into a cocktail shaker and shake vigorously.

You may not be able to eat it with a knife and fork but it should certainly set you up.

John Osborne

A RECIPE FOR HAPPINESS

by Arnold Schwartzman

As a child I fantasized of life amongst the stars in Hollywood. Little did I know that dream would come true and I would end up living there although I must confess that I see more stars at the *White Elephant* than down *Rodeo Drive*. Perhaps there should be a pair of elephant footprints alongside Trigger's in the paving outside Mann's Chinese Theater.

Since the first edition of the White Elephant Celebrity Cook Book a new generation of brilliant illustrators has emerged and so I took the opportunity to invite some of them to add further spice to our pot pourri. They have all contributed their services free in order that some other childhood dreams may come true.

I wish to once again thank Sue Rogers for her dedication to the book's every detail working against time to enable the book to be published at the same time as her own happy event, truly the *Year of the Child!*

ACKNOWLEDGEMENTS

Joe Andrews
John Bernard
Cookie Brusa
Cibachrome
Gerry Collopy
Frank Cock
Tony Evans
Alison Fenton
Face Photosetting
Stephen Garforth
Jim Henson & David Lazer
Tony Hilton
Suzanne Hodgart
Monica Howe
Rosemary Kendall
David Mellor
Phil Meyer
Gilvrie Misstear
Hannah Schwartzman
Barbara Scott
Jocelyn Stevenson
Sheila Stone
Teletape Video

CREDITS

JULIAN ALLEN—ILLUSTRATOR, DONALD PLEASENCE

ENZO APICELLA—ILLUSTRATOR, OMELETTE AU BLE

ROGER BAKER—TYPOGRAPHER

SAUL BASS—DESIGNER, SEA BASS

IAN BECK—ILLUSTRATOR, ICE CREAM CAPRICE

MICHAEL BERKOFSKY—PHOTOGRAPHER, FAY WELDON

PETER BLAKE—ILLUSTRATOR, SHELLEY WINTERS

MARC BOXER—ILLUSTRATOR, DAVID FROST

ALAN BOYD—PHOTOGRAPHER, RONNIE BARKER/GRAPE SPECIAL: SWEDISH GRAVLAX

GLYNN BOYD HARTE—ILLUSTRATOR, AUBERGINES

EVIE BRICUSSE—ILLUSTRATOR, TIMPANA

PETER BROOKES—ILLUSTRATOR, QUEEN VICTORIA/BACON ROLL PUDDING

MICK BROWNFIELD—ILLUSTRATOR, MAX BYGRAVES/SCAMPI

MEL CALMAN—ILLUSTRATOR, POMPEII PUDDING

ROY CARRUTHERS—ILLUSTRATOR, CHICKEN WITH ROSEMARY

PHILIP CASTLE—ILLUSTRATOR, JAMES MASON

LESLIE CHAPMAN—ILLUSTRATOR, BOP

SEYMOUR CHWAST—ILLUSTRATOR, HERMIONE GINGOLD

STEPHEN COE—PHOTOGRAPHER, DIMITRI TIOMKIN

SUE COE—ILLUSTRATOR, JOAN COLLINS

GIANNETTO COPPOLA—ILLUSTRATOR, HARRY ANDREWS

JULIAN COTTRELL—PHOTOGRAPHER, PEACHES IN BRANDY

COLIN CHEESEMAN—ILLUSTRATOR, CHICKEN A LA MAMA CONTI

ALAN CRACKNELL—ILLUSTRATOR, TONY RANDALL/STRAWBERRY DESSERT

PAUL DAVIS—ILLUSTRATOR, BANANA DESSERT

PAULINE ELLISON—ILLUSTRATOR, ERIC SYKES

MICHAEL ENGLISH—ILLUSTRATOR, AVOCADOS GUACAMOLE

TONY EVANS—PHOTOGRAPHER, MAIN TITLES

KENNY EVERETT—ILLUSTRATOR, A CHILLIED TASTE BUD

FACE PHOTOSETTING—DESIGN, WATERCRESS ETCETERA SOUP

ALAN FLETCHER (PENTAGRAM)—DESIGNER, WHITELAW'S GOULASH

MICHAEL FARRELL—ILLUSTRATOR, CHEESE & CUCUMBER MOUSSE

ADRIAN FLOWERS—PHOTOGRAPHER, EDNA O'BRIEN: CAULIFLOWER SOUP

MICHAEL FOREMAN—ILLUSTRATOR, SPIKE MILLIGAN: MOROCCAN CHICKEN PIE

NANCY FOUTS (SHIRTSLEEVE STUDIO)—DESIGNER/PHOTOGRAPHER, FISH PIE:
DESIGNER, VIDAL'S FORK

HARRIET FREEDMAN—ARTIST, CRAB OMELETTE: STUFFED VINE LEAVES

ROB GAGE—PHOTOGRAPHER, 'FISH-PORTER'

JEAN-PAUL GOUDE—ILLUSTRATOR, 'WELSH CAKE'

PATRICK GAVIN—ILLUSTRATOR, JOHNNY MATHIS: LORD GRADE

JOHN GORHAM—ILLUSTRATOR, PICKLED HERRING: COVER DESIGN

NORMAN GREEN—ILLUSTRATOR, DOUBLE FAVOURITE

TERRY GRIFFITHS—ILLUSTRATOR, SALADE COMPOSE

BRIAN GRIMWOOD—ILLUSTRATOR, TURTLE & PEA SOUP: COVER ILLUSTRATION

ROBERT GROSSMAN—ILLUSTRATOR, GLYNIS JOHNS

LARS HAAKONSSEN—ILLUSTRATOR, SEAN CONNERY

GEORGE HARDIE—ILLUSTRATOR, POPPY SEED DRESSING

SAM HASKINS—PHOTOGRAPHER, WENDY CRAIG

DAVID HOLMES—ILLUSTRATOR, JOHN FREEMAN/CHOCOLATE BISCUIT PUDDING

PETER HOWE—PHOTOGRAPHER, RINALDO (MANAGER) & LESLIE CROWTHER:
REGGIE ROSE/CHOPPED LIVER: WILLIS HALL

SU HUNTLEY—ILLUSTRATOR, 'BURGER DINER'

GRAY JOLIFFE—ILLUSTRATOR, FILETS MIGNONS FLAMBES: LELIA GOLDONI

MICHAEL JOSEPH—PHOTOGRAPHER, LESLIE PHILLIPS

JERRY JUHL—WRITER, MISS PIGGY'S FRAISES EAU DISTILLE

LOU KLEIN—DESIGNER, ROGER MOORE

JOHN KOSH—ILLUSTRATOR, KATIE BOYLE/COLD TURKEY

EDDA KOCHL—ILLUSTRATOR, DIANA DORS

LAURENCE KLONARIS—ILLUSTRATOR, FRESH ASPARAGUS

MERVYN KURLANSKY—DESIGNER, CLEO LAINE & JOHN DANKWORTH

BARRY LATEGAN—PHOTOGRAPHER, TWIGGY & JUSTIN/CHRISTMAS PUDDING
(DESIGN: SHIRTSLEEVE STUDIO)

MARTIN LAMBIE-NAIRN—ILLUSTRATOR, QUINN MARTIN/CHICKEN FIESTA

JOHN LAWRENCE-JONES—PHOTOGRAPHER, A CHICKEN

PETER LE VASSEUR—ILLUSTRATOR, RICHARD ATTENBOROUGH

BERNARD LODGE—ILLUSTRATOR, ERIC AMBLER/STUFFED GREEN PEPPER

MAYOTTE MAGNUS—PHOTOGRAPHER, STELLA RICHMAN

ALAN MANHAM—ILLUSTRATOR, ERNIE WISE/FRENCH ONION SOUP

TONY MEEUWISSEN—ILLUSTRATOR, NOAH'S APPLE CAKE

JOHN McCONNELL—DESIGNER, JOHN OSBORNE/BULL SHOT

DONALD McCULLIN—PHOTOGRAPHER, LEE REMICK

STEWART McKINNEN—ILLUSTRATOR, JANSSON'S TEMPTATION

BRUCE McNALLY—ILLUSTRATOR, MISS PIGGY

MARCELLO MINALE—DESIGNER, LEG OF LAMB

SARA MIDDA—ILLUSTRATOR, SHEPHERD'S PIE

GORDON MOORE—PHOTOGRAPHER, NORMAN ROSSINGTON

JEAN MULATIER—ILLUSTRATOR, OLIVER REED

DONNA MUIR—ILLUSTRATOR, GEORGIA BROWN

PATRICIA OLESZKO—ARTIST, DRESSING FOR A 20LB TURKEY (NEIL SELKIRK—
PHOTOGRAPHER: ART DIRECTOR—RICHARD WEIGAND)

HARRI PECCINOTTI—PHOTOGRAPHER, BANANA

DAVID PELHAM—DESIGNER, LEN DEIGHTON: OMAR SHARIF

DAVID POCKNELL—ILLUSTRATOR, JOHN SCHLESINGER/INDIAN KEBABS:
SAMMY DAVIS JNR./LEG OF PORK

NICHOLAS PRICE—ILLUSTRATOR, HERBERT LOM/HAWAIIAN CHICKEN

WILLIAM RANKIN—ILLUSTRATOR, JILL BENNETT

ARTHUR ROBINS—ILLUSTRATOR, ESSEX CURRY

ARNOLD SCHWARTZMAN—ILLUSTRATOR, GERALDO: JOE JANNI/PASTA:
DESIGNER, REGGIE ROSE/CHOPPED LIVER

EDWARD SOREL—ILLUSTRATOR, PETER FINCH

DICK SMITH—ILLUSTRATOR, MILLICENT MARTIN

GILBERT STONE—ILLUSTRATOR, LAURENCE HARVEY

SIMMS TABACK—ILLUSTRATOR, TOPOL

NICK TAGGART—ILLUSTRATOR, ZSA ZSA GABOR

DET. SGT. J. A. TALBOT, NEW SCOTLAND YARD—PHOTO-FIT, SHAW TAYLOR

BRIAN TATTERSFIELD—ILLUSTRATOR, RICOTTA LAYER CAKE

GRAHAM THOMPSON—ILLUSTRATOR, STIRLING MOSS

JOHN TRIBE—ILLUSTRATOR, CHICKEN VINDALOO: CORNISH PASTY

VICKY—ILLUSTRATOR, JACK HAWKINS

JOSEPH WRIGHT—ILLUSTRATOR, RONNIE CORBETT

Metric Equivalents

To the nearest 5 grammes

This chart is intended
as a rough guide only

OUNCES	GRAMMES
1	30
2	55
4	115
6	170
8	225
12	340
16	455

1 teaspoon = 5 millilitres
1 dessertspoon = 10 millilitres
1 tablespoon = 15 millilitres

PINTS	MILLILITRES
$\frac{1}{4}$	142
$\frac{1}{2}$	189
1	568

1 US cup = 8 Imperial fl oz
1 Imperial cup = 10 fl oz

OVEN TEMPERATURES

Gas	Electricity (Fahrenheit)	(Centigrade)
$\frac{1}{4}$–$\frac{1}{2}$	240°F	116°C
1	275°F	135°C
2	290°F	144°C
3	325°F	163°C
4	350°F	177°C
5	375°F	190°C
6	400°F	200°C
7	425°F	218°C
8	450°F	232°C
9	475°F	246°C

INDEX

YOUR OWN WHITE ELEPHANTS

YOUR OWN WHITE ELEPHANTS

YOUR OWN WHITE ELEPHANTS

YOUR OWN WHITE ELEPHANTS

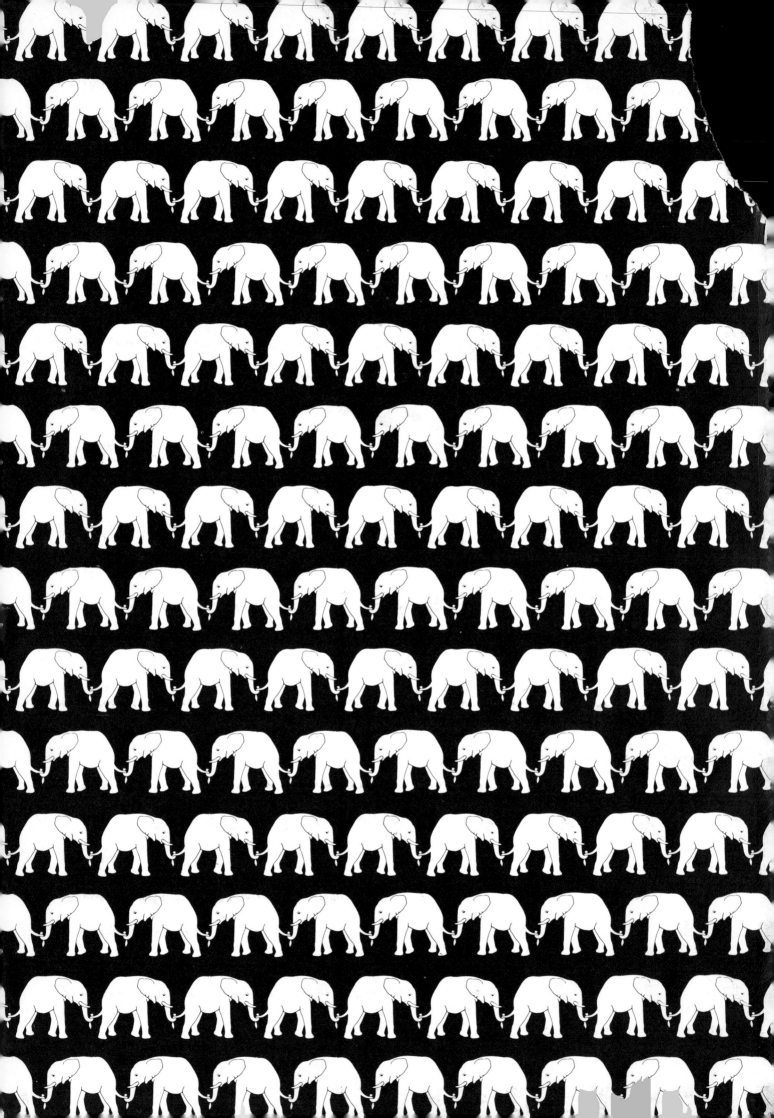